COPING WITH SEXUAL ABUSE

JUDITH COONEY, Ed.D.

THE ROSEN PUBLISHING GROUP

NEW YORK

Published in 1987, 1991 by The Rosen Publishing Group, Inc.
29 East 21st Street, New York, NY 10010

Revised Edition 1991

Library of Congress Cataloging-in Publication Data

Cooney, Judith.
  Coping with sexual abuse.

  Includes index.
  Summary: Discusses the myths and effects of
sexual abuse, treatment of victims, and ways to
prevent such abuse.
  1. Child molesting—United States—Juvenile
literature.   2. Child molesting—United States—
Prevention—Juvenile literature.   3. Sexually
abused children—United States—Juvenile literature.
[1. Child molesting.   2. Child abuse]   I. Title.
HQ72.U53C66   1987   362.7'044   86-29641
ISBN 0-8239-1336-8

Manufactured in the United States of America

Contents

About the Author

Judith Cooney is a professor in the Division of Psychology and Counseling, Governors State University, University Park, Illinois. She teaches a variety of counseling courses, including a course in physical and sexual abuse of children. Prior to teaching at Governors State, Dr. Cooney was an elementary school counselor in Deerfield, Illinois.

Dr. Cooney has conducted workshops on various aspects of child abuse throughout the United States, Canada, and Australia. She has been a Parents Anonymous sponsor, a group leader for battered women, and a hospital emergency room volunteer. Her study of child abuse began in the doctoral program at Indiana University.

Dr. Cooney's interests include spectator sports, travel, and reading. She is active in child protection and animal protection organizations. She resides in Crete, Illinois, and is the owner of a formerly abused shepherd/collie.

Introduction to the Second Edition

Since this book was first published in 1987, the longest and most costly sexual abuse case in the United States has come to an end. I am referring to the McMartin preschool case in California. In 1984 grand jury indictments had been handed down against seven teachers, six of whom were women. As the case was played out over the next six years, national television coverage familiarized people with previously unknown aspects of sexual abuse and its consequences. No longer could the stereotype of the "dirty old man" hold up. Paraded across the screen on the evening news were white, middle-class women, including a 77-year-old grandmother wearing a Snoopy pin.

The legal proceedings cost California taxpayers $13.5 million. The last defendant, grandson of the school's founder, was acquitted in July 1990. No convictions resulted from the McMartin case. The emotional cost to all the children who testified and to their parents cannot be measured in dollars, nor in hours of therapy.

Those who were inclined to dismiss the McMartin case as something that could happen only in California had more difficulty dismissing a concurrent case in the heartland of the United States. Jordan, Minnesota, a suburb of Minneapolis, seemed an unlikely locale for the notoriety associated with large-scale sexual abuse. Again the accused shattered the stereotype. Twenty-four men and women, including married couples, police officers, and teachers, were arrested in a case that included animal sacrifices and hints of a murdered child.

Despite the absence of convictions in this and the McMartin cases, the resulting publicity and discussion brought about a greater understanding of sexual abuse. The public became more aware that the crime of sexual abuse can occur anywhere and be perpetrated by people who seem trustworthy and successful by community standards.

Another concern that has been brought to public attention by means of a court case is the sexual abuse of children by noncustodial parents in divorced families. A case involving Dr. Elizabeth Morgan, a physician and mother, is indicative of the turmoil created in such situations. Convinced that her young daughter was being molested during visits to the child's father, Dr. Morgan refused to permit further visits. When the court ordered her to comply with the visitation schedule, she refused to reveal her daughter's whereabouts. Dr. Morgan was jailed while police searched unsuccessfully for her daughter. As the months of confinement turned into years, questions about children's rights, parental rights, and sexual abuse as a divorce issue remained unresolved.

Court cases have forced the public to come to terms with the reality of sexual abuse and the inadequacy of the legal system to protect children. Greater public awareness has been one of the changes since the publication of this book. Another change has been the painful realization that adolescents are not only the victims of sexual abuse, but also sometimes the victimizers. We are just beginning to acknowledge the presence of adolescent offenders in sexual abuse. A chapter has been added to address that phenomenon. A final chapter encouraging adolescent involvement in prevention has also been included.

It is hoped that first-time readers will find this book enlightening and challenging. It is also hoped that second-time readers may gain new knowledge that will lead to positive action to protect children from sexual abuse.

CHAPTER I

Sexual Abuse: An Introduction

This book deals with a topic that makes many people uncomfortable. Until recently the sexual abuse of children and adolescents has been a subject rarely mentioned in newspapers, on television, or in schools. No one likes to think about a child being forced to do sexual things; least of all do we want to acknowledge that it happens to all ages, including infants and toddlers.

Every year in the United States thousands of cases of sexual abuse of children are reported to police departments and child protection agencies. Authorities estimate that one out of four girls and one out of seven boys will be sexually abused or molested before age eighteen. When we apply those statistics to an average-sized classroom, the numbers take on a new meaning. It is realistic to consider the probability that someone you know is a victim of sexual abuse. By reading and thinking about this problem, you may learn to help a friend or family member to whom this is happening. You may also learn to protect yourself from becoming a victim. Most important, it is my hope that this book can help you identify some alternatives to stop the abuse.

As you read this book, some things may confuse you or frighten you. It is possible that one of the situations that are described will remind you of something that happened to you in the past or is happening to you now. It is essential that you talk over your questions, concerns, or reactions with someone who will take the time to listen.

In school, that helping person might be your school counselor, social worker, or favorite teacher. At home it might be a parent, an older brother or sister, or another relative. If the person you choose has difficulty talking about sexual abuse, don't give up! Unfortunately, some people believe that not talking about something troublesome will make it go away. If you encounter this attitude regarding sexual abuse, keep bringing up the subject with responsible adults until you get help. Counselors and social workers know that talking about a concern is the first step in doing something about it.

WHAT IS SEXUAL ABUSE?

Every state has laws that prohibit sexual conduct with children and adolescents. Although these laws vary in details from state to state, they agree for the most part on what constitutes behavior that is sexually abusive. Sexual abuse is the use of a child or an adolescent for sexual activity.

Let us look at what this definition says and does not say. We know from the definition that a minor is the victim in sexual abuse. A minor is defined differently from state to state. Most frequently, a minor is defined as a person aged seventeen or younger. Thus victims of sexual abuse may range from infants to high school seniors. The use of someone in this age range for sexual activity must be clarified. Just as we are considering a variety of ages, we are considering a variety of activities that are sexual in nature. Often people think that sexual abuse refers only to sexual intercourse. Certainly sexual intercourse with a minor is a form of sexual abuse. However, many victims of sexual abuse do not have intercourse with their abuser. Instead they may experience genital exposure, fondling, forced touching, inappropriate kissing, or oral sex. They may be forced to watch others engage in sexual activities. Some examples of sexual abuse will clarify the nature of these offenses.

A. Elizabeth is ten. Her father comes into her room when she is sleeping and pulls her nightgown up so that he can rub her genital area with his hands.

B. Jimmy is two. His mother keeps him in her bed and masturbates him until he has an erection.

C. Steve and his friend Bob are invited to play video games at a neighbor's house. While playing, the neighbor suggests that the boys have a naked wrestling match while he takes pictures of them.

D. Andrea has been thinking about running away from home; her mother's boyfriend tries to kiss her and take off her clothes while her mother is at work.

E. Sally's teacher asks her to stay after class. While he is talking to her, he puts his arm around her and starts fondling her breast.

F. Bonnie's parents are divorced. Her father has been having intercourse with her since she was eleven. Her mother doesn't understand why she is reluctant to stay overnight at her father's new apartment.

G. Carl is fifteen. He baby-sits for his six-year-old niece. He gets into bed with her and makes her rub his penis.

H. Tom's stepmother insists on giving him a bath, even though he is ten. She takes off her clothes and gets into the tub with him.

These are a few of hundreds of examples of sexually abusive behavior. In each, we see a person in authority taking advantage of someone markedly younger and less powerful. Sometimes "in authority" means just being an adult, as in Example C. Children are taught to do what adults tell them to do. People who sexually abuse children rely on the fact that children have learned to obey.

In these examples we see that abusers can be either male or female, that they may select a victim of the same sex or of the opposite sex, and that they may be a family member, a friend, or an acquaintance. Sometimes the abuser is also a minor, as in the case of Carl with his niece.

THE MOLESTER

One kind of example was not used. That is the type of attack that children are warned about when they are young. Most of us remember being told to stay away from the bushes in the park, not to talk to strangers, and never, under any circumstances, to get in a car with a stranger. At the time we were probably given no reasons for these rules. As we grew older we realized that the stranger might be a child molester.

The advice was good advice. There are people who sexually attack children randomly. However, eighty percent of all reports of sexual abuse involve an abuser who is known and trusted by the child. Strangers do indeed molest or abuse children. However, eight out of ten times the abuser is not the "bogeyman" hiding in the bushes. It is instead a parent, a stepparent, a grandparent, an uncle, an aunt, a cousin, a neighbor, a family friend, a teacher, a clergyman, or someone else who has easy access to the victim.

In schools we do a good job of warning children about strangers. We are just beginning to teach them that the person to worry about may be a family member or trusted friend. In this book we focus on that eighty percent person, not the molester who victimizes children anonymously and disappears. However, some important things must be considered about the molester before we move on to our primary emphasis.

The child molester, or more scientifically, the pedophile, is a person whose major interest in life is to find children to use for sexual gratification. Most of the time molesters are male. Their victims may be male or female. Because they are constantly seeking new victims, molesters frequent areas where children are available. Such places as parks, playgrounds, schools, movie theaters, shopping malls, arcades, and carnivals are favorite places to search for potential victims.

PEDOPHILES

Pedophiles use a variety of tricks to persuade children or adolescents to go with them. Some pretend to be a friend of a child's parents who has been sent to give the child a ride home. Some pretend to need assistance in finding directions or a missing puppy. Others promise a reward of candy or money or drugs. Whatever the ruse, the motive remains the same: to engage the child or adolescent in sexual activity.

Sometimes pedophiles use physical force to get what they want. More often they use threats of harm to keep their victim from telling anyone what has happened. They may say things like, "I'll come back and kill you if you tell," or, "I know where you live and I'll be waiting for you."

An attack by a molester is a very frightening experience. The victim may be confused about what has happened and fearful that his parents will be angry. The molester counts on his victim's being too upset or terrified to tell the parents. Because the child may have broken parental rules by getting into a stranger's car or by being where he or she was not supposed to be, the child fears parental anger and does not report the attack.

Despite the consequences, it is important that the victim of a molester tell a parent or someone in authority as soon as possible after the attack. The sooner a report is made to the police, the more likely it is that the molester will still be in the vicinity where he can be caught. Not reporting such an attack makes it possible for the molester to continue victimizing others.

THE MOLESTER VS. THE SEXUAL ABUSER

You may be wondering about the differences between a molester and a sexual abuser. An attack by a molester differs from sexual abuse in the following ways:

1. *Relationship to the victim.* The anonymous molester encounters the child once and moves on. In sexual abuse there is usually an ongoing relationship in which the victim sees the abuser periodically.
2. *Physical harm.* The molester is more likely to use physical harm or the threat of harm to control his victim. Some sexual abusers also threaten harm to their victims, but they are more inclined to use emotional blackmail involving other people. For example, the sexual abuser might say, "If you tell your mother she'll have a heart attack and it will be your fault," or, "If you tell anyone there will be a divorce and you'll all have to move out of the house."
3. *Duration.* An encounter with a molester is a one-time experience. Sexual abuse usually occurs over a pro-

longed period of time; the victim may be victimized for months or years by the same abuser.
4. *Reporting.* The molester is much more likely to be reported to the police than is the sexual abuser. Parents and victims are more willing to report a stranger than they are a member of the family or a family friend.
5. *Effects.* A sexual attack by a stranger or continued abuse by a trusted adult are both traumatic and may require extensive counseling. Because the attack by the molester was a single occurrence, it may have fewer long-lasting emotional effects on the victim than does the ongoing sexual abuse.
6. *Support.* Usually in instances of sexual molestation by a stranger the family and friends of the victim are supportive and comforting. This support helps the victim deal with the attack and put the experience in the past. In the case of sexual abuse, the abuser may be a family member. The relationship may result in divided loyalties within the family; the victim may feel deserted and rejected.
7. *Treatment.* The molester or pedophile is a threat to all children; the sexual abuser within a family usually limits his victims to family members. This is particularly important when treatment is considered. Many pedophiles are never caught. The ones who are caught may be fined, or serve a brief term in jail, or both. Once they are free, they return to preying on children. Unfortunately, counseling does not seem to be effective with pedophiles. The opposite is true with abusers.

THE COMBINATION MOLESTER/ SEXUAL ABUSER

Sometimes the pedophile is also a sexual abuser. That

may seem strange, especially since we've just considered some of the differences between the pedophile and the sexual abuser. The story of Harold may clarify the point.

Harold is a salesman. His territory includes four states. He travels through his territory by car, stopping in many small towns to call on customers. His schedule is very flexible. He is friendly and talkative and prides himself on dressing well. Harold is a pedophile. As he travels, he looks for children in parks or isolated areas. Sometimes he tells them that he is looking for his nephew and needs their help. Other times he pretends to be lost and asks for directions. As he talks he attempts to get his victims to walk with him into a secluded area. When they follow him, he molests them. Before he leaves he tells them that he will be watching and they must stay right where they are for fifteen minutes or they'll "be sorry." He hurries to his car and leaves town, probably before the victim has moved from the spot where Harold left him.

Harold travels from town to town, working and molesting children all week. He spends weekends at home with his family. Last year he married a woman with four young children. He met his wife at a club for single parents. Harold went to that club specifically to meet someone who had children. He molests his stepchildren when he is at home. He is a sexual abuser.

No one knows how many "Harolds" there are. We do know that they are a threat to all children, their own and everyone else's. Some experts believe that all sexual abusers are pedophiles. Others believe that there are many pedophiles, many sexual abusers, and a relatively few combination pedophile/sexual abusers.

Our focus in this book is on the sexual abuser, a person known and trusted by his victim.

THE SEXUAL ABUSER

The majority of sexual abusers are males. The most typical sexual abuse situation is one in which the father sexually abuses his daughter or stepdaughter. The next most common case is one in which the father abuses his son or stepson. Next in order of reports comes sibling abuse, in which a brother or sister sexually abuses a younger brother or sister. As in father-daughter sexual abuse, the usual pattern in sibling abuse is that an older brother victimizes a younger sister. In some instances the victim is a younger brother.

A rarer occurrence than any other is sexual abuse by the mother of a victim. In this situation the victim is more likely to be a male than a female. Cases have been reported in which a child was sexually abused by both parents.

Other family members may also be sexual abusers. Again, it is more likely that these abusers are male, that is, an uncle, a grandfather, or a male cousin. Sexual abuse of family members is often referred to as incest.

In addition to the anonymous molester and the family member is the abuser who is a trusted family friend or caretaker for the victim. In this category might be neighbors, day-care workers, teachers, clergy, doctors, baby-sitters, coaches, Scout leaders, and anyone else to whose care the child or adolescent might be entrusted.

As you can tell from the lengthy list of potential abusers, there is no clear-cut set of characteristics that would help us identify abusers. They come from all races and religions, all educational and career levels, all age categories and socio-economic levels. What they have in common is easy access to their victims. They are usually in a position of authority and use that authority to control their victims.

The Father

The vast majority of sexual abuse cases involve a father who is abusing his daughter or daughters. It is possible that as a child or adolescent he was sexually abused. You might think that the pain of his own experience would make it unlikely that he would inflict abuse on anyone else. However, the reverse seems to occur. As a victim he was controlled by someone else. He identifies with that attacker and seeks to exert the same kind of control over others.

As a husband he may be very dependent on a domineering wife. He may leave everthing to his wife to decide. She complains that she feels more like his mother than his wife. He feels inadequate and angry. He turns to his children for nurturing and attention.

Another possible pattern is just the opposite of the dependent husband. This father is a tyrant. He considers his wife and children his possessions. He controls everything. His relationship with his wife is similar to a father-daughter relationship. His authority is never questioned by other family members. He believes that his family exists solely to meet his needs.

The Mother

In some sexual abuse cases the mother is physically or emotionally absent from the family. She may be deceased or chronically ill. She may suffer from emotional problems that keep her from participation in the family. In some instances the daughter takes on the role of wife that her mother cannot fulfill.

In families where the wife is domineering, she may have the role of both father and mother. Her dependent husband functions more as a child than as an adult. In families where the husband is a tyrant, the wife may take a very passive role. She probably does not drive, does not work, does not make decisions, and is totally dependent on her husband. Her husband rules the family, and she does not dare to question his rules and expectations.

Some wives of men who sexually abuse their children were sexually abused as children themselves. They grew up believing that such abuse was a normal happening in a family. They are not surprised when history repeats itself and their own children are victimized.

The Family

Just as there is no one set of absolute characteristics for parents in a sexual abuse situation, there is no clearly defined definition of the family in which abuse takes place. Some generalizations, however, seem to apply in many cases. One is that the marital relationship is poor. This may not be apparent to outsiders, who may consider the parents a very happy couple. The children are likely to be aware of the "nonrelationship" that exists. Another characteristic of the abusive family is that communication among members is limited. Nothing of importance is discussed; least of all is sex a topic. If anything, the family may seem prudish and extremely moral to observers. Often the husband and wife are repeating the patterns of their own childhood.

Sexual abuse is a symptom of a family in crisis. Many things are wrong in such a family; sexual abuse is only one of them. In addition to the poor marital relationship, there may be conflict with other family members or neighbors, financial difficulties, health problems, or other stressful factors. If such a family is to be helped, they need assistance in many areas, not just with the sexual abuse issue.

SUMMARY

This chapter has presented an overview of sexual abuse. The term sexual abuse is not synonymous with sexual intercourse. It includes a variety of sexual activities involving a minor. While children have long been warned of the stranger danger, in reality the abuser is more likely to be an acquaintance or a family member than a stranger.

The differences between molesters and sexual abusers were discussed. Finally, a more detailed description of the father, the mother, and the family in sexual abuse was presented.

DISCUSSION TOPICS

1. React to the statistics that indicate that one of four girls and one of seven boys will be victims of sexual abuse or attack. Apply those numbers to your class; to your school.
2. Return to the examples of sexual abuse. Which children were victims of an abuser? of a pedophile? How can you tell?
3. "Harold" may come to your neighborhood. Role-play some responses to him.
4. What would you want to teach your younger brother or sister to protect them from a molester? from an abuser in your family?
5. Discuss some ideas as to why more men than women are molesters and sexual abusers.
6. If you could plan a school assembly about sexual abuse, what information would be most helpful to other students?

CHAPTER II

Myths Related to Sexual Abuse

A myth is a story used to explain the unexplainable, to make sense out of things that make no sense. Sometimes people use myths to protect themselves from painful reality. There are many myths associated with sexual abuse, because the reality of the problem is incomprehensible and frightening to many. The most popular of all the myths is that the abuser is some furry-faced creature lurking in the bushes. Let us examine that myth more closely.

Myth #1: The sexual abuser is usually a stranger to his victim.

Reality: Eighty percent of the time the sexual abuser is someone known and trusted by his victim. Rather than attacking from the bushes, the abuser uses his authority position to control and manipulate his victim. Because he has time to develop a relationship with his victim, he is able to identify and use the victim's needs, interests, and desires to his own advantage. For example, a father may provide all the material comforts that his family requires, but he may not be inclined to demonstrate any affection toward his children. Thus the children live in an emotionally sterile environment. If he begins to bestow affection on one of his daughters, it is understandable that she would welcome this new and needed dimension in their relationship. Over a period of time the father may take advantage of her longing for affection and overstep the boundaries that separate fatherly love from abuse. He has misused his daughter's need for affection.

As another example, a favorite uncle, knowing his nephew's love of baseball, begins taking the boy to games. He may also buy the boy various baseball paraphernalia. Eventually he may ask the boy to do sexual things to him while driving him home from the games. The boy feels indebted, trapped, and confused. The uncle has capitalized on the boy's baseball interest to develop a strong bond that the boy does not want to destroy.

As was said in Chapter I, concern about being molested by a stranger is legitimate. Strangers do molest children. But the image of the molester is often unreal. A molester who looked strange and frightening would fail to persuade children to trust him. The molester makes every attempt to blend into his surroundings. To do otherwise would jeopardize his chances for entrapping victims.

Myth #2: If the sexual abuser is the father of the victim, he is actually a stepparent.

Reality: In father-daughter and father-son sexual abuse, the natural father is most likely to be the abuser. Certainly stepfathers, stepmothers, and parents' boyfriends or girlfriends may be sexually abusive. However, the more common case is that of the natural parent being the abuser.

Many people find comfort in the stepparent myth. It somehow seems more acceptable to think that the abuser is less closely related to his victim.

This same solace has helped to perpetuate the stranger myth. Painful as it may be to consider, when the boundaries between father and abuser are crossed, it is most likely to be the natural father who crosses them.

Myth #3: Some children are naturally seductive and encourage adult sexual attention.

Reality: The victim is never at fault in sexual abuse. The myth of the seductive child is a particularly cruel one. It implies that the child is responsible for the adult's behavior. Just the opposite is true. A child who seems sexually knowledgeable beyond his/her years, who approaches adults sexually, or who dresses in an adult manner has been taught that the way to receive attention is by acting out sexually.

Children are not naturally seductive. They want and need affection and attention from the adults in their world. They may emulate adult behavior to get that attention. The prudent parent discourages "femme fatale" or Romeo behavior if it emerges. Abusive parents may encourage and actually train children to act "sexy" for a variety of reasons. One might be to help them justify their sexual involvement with that child. The parents rationalize their abusive behavior by telling themselves that the child is really a mini-adult who desires their sexual advances. Another, less common reason for training a child to behave sexually is that a parent may want to exploit the child for financial gain. Sadly, there are parents who profit from the child pornography and child prostitution markets. Children have been forced into prostitution to support a parent's drug habit. Others have been used in child pornography magazines or movies produced by their parents. All of these children are victims of their parents, not instigators of the adult's sexual behavior.

Myth #4: A parent would have to be drunk, on drugs, or crazy to molest his own son or daughter.

Reality: The sexually abusive parent is usually considered a model citizen. This is a very comforting myth. The majority of the adult population is not alcoholic, on drugs, or crazy. By identifying sexual abuse with these social problems, people are really saying, "The sexual abuser is different from me, from my family members, and from people I know." In addition, there is an implication that anyone who sexually abuses his/her child cannot be "in his right mind."

Some abusers do misuse drugs or alcohol. There is no indication that drug or alcohol abuse is any greater among sexual abusers than among the "normal" population. Alcohol or drugs do not cause sexual abuse. However, if caught, an abuser may blame drugs or alcohol for what he has done. This is a convenient way of rejecting responsibility for one's own behavior. Many people use drugs or alcohol but do not abuse their children. Alcohol abuse, drug abuse, and sexual abuse are separate problems; one does not cause the other.

With the recent addition of certain behavioral categories, it has been estimated that ten to fifteen percent of the United States population could be considered to be suffering from mental illness. There is no research to indicate that the percentages are any different for sexual abusers than for the general population.

Most sexual abusers function in their jobs, vote, attent church, and from all appearances seem to be model citizens. Their families take up much of their leisure time. If they participate in outside activities, the activities tend to be child- or family-related.

Myth #5: Sexual abuse is a twentieth-century phenomenon.

Reality: From the beginning of written history, sexual abuse has been recorded. In ancient Rome and Greece, child prostitution was socially acceptable. Boys in particular were victimized by adult men. Brother-sister marriages were common in ancient Egypt, India, Persia, and Peru. The marriages were viewed as insurance to guarantee that the family riches would not have to be shared with outsiders. The Bible refers to sexual relationships between Lot and his daughters; Noah and his son; and the sons of Adam and Eve, Cain and Abel, with their twin sisters. The Middle Ages contributed a long list of kings and popes involved in incestuous relationships. Incest was an accepted practice in some groups through the end of the nineteenth century in the United States.

Sexual abuse cannot be blamed on the industrial revolution or on technological advances. It cannot be blamed on the drug culture or a permissive society. Throughout history children have been considered the property of their parents. Parents had the right to do whatever they chose to do to their own children. They could sell them as slaves, apprentice them to anyone willing to pay the price, maim them and put them on the streets to beg, or kill them if they became unruly. Laws to protect children have not ended abuse. The exploitation of children continues in more subtle ways than in the past.

Myth #6: Sexual abuse is rare.

Reality: One out of four girls and one out of seven boys will be sexually victimized by the age of eighteen. No one knows the exact number of victims of childhood sexual abuse. What we do know is that each year in the United States the number of re ported cases increases. It has been estimated that for every case of sexual abuse that is reported, ten cases go unreported. As an example, last year in Illinois there were over 9,500 reports of sexual abuse of children. If ten times that many actual cases occurred, we would estimate that there were 95,000 cases of sexual abuse in Illinois. If we apply that formula to the other forty-nine states, we would say that sexual abuse cases number, not in the thousands, but in the hundreds of thousands each year.

Every state has a law requiring certain people, referred to as mandated reporters, to report suspected cases of physical or sexual abuse to child protection authorities. In most states these man dated reporters include doctors, teachers, coun selors, law enforcement officers, and others who have contact with children. In addition, any concerned citizen, including a victim of abuse, may report to the state agency. Physical abuse, because of obvious bruises and welts, is more likely to be reported than is sexual abuse. Because the injuries in sexual abuse are primarily emotional rather than physical, it is less likely that someone other than the victim will be aware of the abuse. Unless the victim tells someone, the sexual abuse will not be reported and the victim will continue to be victimized.

Myth #7: Child sexual abuse is not harmful to children.
Reality: Sexual abuse of children causes long-lasting emotional problems. When sexual abuse cases come to the attention of authorities, the father or other perpetrator may claim that no harm has been done. The abuser may point out that no bones have been broken, no one has been physically hurt, and no one is damaged by the abuse. The truth is that for some victims there is physical damage ranging from tissue damage and internal bleeding to venereal disease. Most common, however, are the emotional problems that result from sexual abuse. Young victims sometimes experience sleep problems, nightmares, nervous reactions such as nail-biting and tics, learning difficulties, fear of adults, depression, and loss of self-esteem. Adolescents may experience similar problems as well as behavior difficulties. Because of their sexual experiences, they may feel older than their peers. They may have trouble fitting in with others of their age and become loners. They

may experience a deep sense of shame and guilt. Sometimes they attempt to escape the pain by running away, misuse of drugs or alcohol, promiscuous or delinquent behavior, or suicide.

With the AIDS epidemic, a new threat to sexually abused children must be confronted: that a victim may contract AIDS from an abuser. In a court case in southern Illinois a six-year-old was molested by a relative who was infected with the HIV virus. With no cure known for AIDS, the child may have received a death sentence. In other words, a child who is abused by a parent beginning at age five or six and continuing into adolescence is more likely to suffer extreme effects of sexual abuse than is a child abused by a neighbor at age twelve on two occasions. Neither situation is harmless; one may be less harmful than the other.

Myth #8: Families in which there is sexual abuse are normal, happy families in every other way.

Reality: Sexual abuse is a symptom of a troubled family. Families in which sexual abuse is occurring may give the impression to the outside world that everything is fine. The victim is told by the abuser that he or she is helping to keep the family together. The reality is that sexual abuse does not occur in normal, happy families. Many things are not all right in an abusive family. The relationship between the parents is usually poor. They may have no physical relationship and little emotional contact.

They are strangers living under the same roof. If they communicate at all, it is often in the form of criticizing or arguing. The children living in such a household would agree that they would not want a marriage like their parents'. Communication between parents and children is also poor, as is the communication between the children. No one talks with anyone in the family with any depth. A state of tension exists in the household that is accepted as the way families are.

There may be other kinds of stress in such a family, including financial problems, job problems, and problems with neighbors or other relatives. If reported, family members will need help with many other concerns in addition to sexual abuse.

Myth #9: When sexual abuse occurs in the family, it is a secret shared by only the victim and the abuser.

Reality: The longer the abuse goes on, the more likely it is that others in the household know that it is occurring. Have you ever tried to keep a secret from a brother or sister or parent? If so, you probably have not been very successful. People who live together tend to notice even slight changes in the behavior or habits of those around them. The longer sexual abuse goes on, the less likely it is that it will remain a secret. Brothers and sisters are aware that a child has become a parent's favorite. The abuser may send other children outside to play or on errands to insure that he will be alone with his victim. If a child returns too soon, he or she may actually witness an abusive situation or

may be made painfully aware that he is not supposed to be there. Even young children deduce
that there is more to the "errand" than appears.
While the brothers or sisters may not know specifically what is occurring, they are aware that something is happening between a parent and sibling
that is a secret, not to be mentioned or questioned.
The favored status of the victim plus the secrecy of
the abuser-victim contacts will not always add up
to a conscious awareness of the sexual nature of
the relationship, but will lead to an awareness that
something "not right" is going on.

The awareness of the other parent, most often
the mother, in sexual abuse is a topic of much
debate. Sometimes sexual abuse occurs when the
mother is absent. If she is hospitalized, deceased,
or living away from her spouse, she would not
know of the abuse. However, in most cases both
parents are residing in the home. Just as with
siblings, the longer the abuse goes on, the more
difficult it is for the mother not to sense that the
relationship between her spouse and child is inappropriate. For a variety of reasons the mother may
feel that she cannot intervene on behalf of the
child.

Sexual abuse is a secret, but it is a family secret
rather than one known only to the child and the
abuser.

Myth #10: Sexual abuse is a response to a need for sexual
gratification.
Reality: Sexual abuse is a response to many needs. If a
father were only seeking sexual gratification with

someone other than his spouse, a variety of adult resources would be available to him outside the family. The question of why a father would turn to his daughter or son for sexual pleasure is not easy to answer. For some, the issue may be one of power or control. If an abuser considers his children to be his property, he has the power to do whatever he likes with them. He may feel that only at home is he in charge; he exerts his power in the only place where he is the boss.

For others, sexual involvement with a child is the angriest act one can commit against the spouse. The major problem lies in the relationship between the husband and wife; the child is incidental. That fact is verified by the father who sexually abuses all of his daughters or all of his sons. He has not fallen in love with each one of them. He is simply using each one to fulfill his need for power or to express anger or to find nurturance. The sexual abuser focuses solely on his own needs and rationalizes away those of his victims.

Myth #11: Minors, particularly adolescents, make up stories of sexual abuse.
Reality: It is extremely unlikely that minors will lie about sexual abuse.

Every child has conflicts with parents. The adolescent years may be especially difficult as teenagers strive for more independence. Rules and parental values come into question. Teens may feel that parents are too restrictive and unfair. Often teens feel that parents do not understand them. Most children and teenagers have ways of getting even with their parents for real or imagined wrongs. Poor performance in school, selecting friends certain to meet with parental disapproval, throwing tantrums, staying in their room, not participating in family activities, not speaking to family members, or getting involved with drugs or alcohol are some ways that teens get back at parents. Any of these behaviors carried to an extreme may signal a disturbed family relationship. Family counseling may be required to change these patterns.

It is a big step from those behaviors, however, to accusing a parent or parent figure of sexual abuse. Let us consider the repercussions of such a charge. When sexual abuse comes to the attention of a mandated reporter, that person must make the accusation known to an office of the state protection service agency. In many states that agency will notify the local police department of the charge.

The victim will have to repeat the details of the abuse to an investigator. The story may have to be repeated for still others. The victim will have to discuss intimate information with a series of strangers. That can be a very uncomfortable experience.

The accused abuser may be removed from the home and arrested. The victim may be placed in a foster home while the investigation is going on. It would be extremely difficult to stand by a false accusation with all of these factors to consider.

Reality is that it takes a great deal of courage for victims of sexual abuse to come forward. When they do share their secret with someone, they should be believed. If the abuse did not occur, discrepancies in the repeated story will begin to surface. The made-up charge, though rare, cannot be ignored. It is an indication of a severe parent-child relationship problem. Counseling is an absolute necessity in such cases.

Myth #12: Sexual abuse is mainly a problem for girls.
Reality: One out of seven boys will be sexually abused before reaching age eighteen. It is true that the most common sexual abuse situation is that of a father molesting his daughter. However, the second most prevalent situation is a father molesting his son. The major reason that we hear or read less about boys who are sexually abused is that boys are less likely than girls to report the abuse. Added to the fear and guilt that girls may feel about being victimized is the fact that boys are usually molested by males. The boys may wrongly think that because of the molestation they are homosexuals. They may think that if they tell anyone they will be labeled "gay." If a boy is molested by a female, he may still be reluctant to report the abuse. He fears that in our macho society he will be ridiculed for complaining about what may be perceived by some as an opportunity rather than an abusive situation.

Sexual abuse is just as real for boys as it is for girls. It must be recognized that forced sexual activity is not acceptable under any circumstances, regardless of the sex of the victim or of the abuser.

SUMMARY

In this chapter some of the most common myths regarding sexual abuse have been cited. We shall examine some of them more closely in other sections. They are significant because belief in such myths prevents the development of effective programs for the prevention and remediation of sexual abuse.

DISCUSSION TOPICS

1. Identify other myths related to sexual abuse.
2. What are some ways that you can tell someone is a believer in a myth or several myths about sexual abuse? How would you deal with such a person?
3. Identify a myth that you thought was true until you read this chapter. What do you think about that myth now? Share this reaction with a partner.
4. Role-play dealing with someone who says that sexual abuse is only something done by strangers, never by parents or other family members.
5. Watch for reports of sexual abuse in newspapers. What myths do these stories support? Which myths are not supported by these reports?
6. Which of the myths do you wish were true? Why?
7. How do you think these myths affect the handling of sexual abuse cases? How do they affect public attitudes toward the problem?

CHAPTER III

Girls as Victims

In this chapter we shall take a closer look at the victimization of a girl by her father. This is the most common pattern of child sexual abuse. Although we shall examine a specific example, it is important to realize there are many variations of this experience. For some girls the abuse begins at an early age; for others it begins later. For some it may go on for ten or more years. It may even continue after the daughter has moved away from home. For others it may continue for less than a year. The abuser is not always a parent. It may be an uncle, a cousin, an aunt, a sister, brother, or grandfather. Regardless of the specific details, sexual abuse of daughters seems to progress through several stages. Let us first look at those stages and then apply them to a typical case of father-daughter sexual abuse.

THE BEGINNING OR ENCOUNTER PERIOD

There is no specific time limit to the encounter period. The abuser chooses a daughter to be his special child. Usually he selects the eldest daughter still living at home. She may be a toddler or a preschooler. She may be in elementary school. Usually she is not older than ten in the beginning stage. Nothing sexual may occur for weeks or even months. The father merely treats this daughter differently than his other children. He may take her places where the others in the family do not go. He may even take her on overnight trips or camping expeditions. If he is severe with his other children, he is more gentle with her. He may be physically abusive to his other children, but not to this daughter. Not only does he give her extra time, but he also may buy her presents or give her money. The girl responds very positively to the extra attention and special treatment from her father. She does not want to go back to the way things used to be when she had little attention or nurturing from him.

At some point, while giving her affection he may slip his hand inside her underwear. She is surprised by the action and may pull away. Her father reassures her that he cares about her and everything is all right. There may be no other sexual advance for days or weeks. The daughter assumes that what happened was an accident and that things between her and her father are back to normal. Then it happens again.

THE ENGAGEMENT PERIOD

When her father approaches her the second time, the daughter is more confused than surprised. He is gentle with her and reassures her that he loves her and will not hurt her. From this time on, sexual demands tend to become more frequent. He may now begin coming into her room at night. She may wake up to find him lifting her nightgown and touching her genital area. She is frightened and confused by what is going on. He is her father, whom she is supposed to obey and trust. Fathers take care of their children. Her "protector" keeps telling her that what he is doing to her is "O.K." But if it is "O.K." why does he keep warning her not to tell anyone what they do when they're together?

Her father becomes more and more demanding. When she protests, the gentleness is his voice disappears, to be replaced by threats. These threats might not make much sense to an adult, but the victim is not an adult. He tells her anything that he thinks she will believe. His goal is twofold: to keep her from telling anyone about his behavior and to convince her that she must continue to cooperate. He may threaten her with harm to herself. "If you tell anyone you'll be sent to reform school." He may threaten others: "If you don't do this I'll divorce your mother, and you kids will all go to foster homes. Is that what you want?" Or, "If you tell anyone, your mother will kill herself. It will be your fault." These are very real threats to a child. She feels trapped. There is no way out. She becomes convinced that she has no choice but to submit to his ever-escalating demands. Her safety and the safety of other family members depend on her silent submission.

This phase may go on for years. The victim does what she is told. She tries not to think about anything when her father "visits" her. She masturbates him, has oral sex with him, does anything he requires of her, and waits for a time when she can be free of him. For many victims, this stage lasts until they leave home. For others there is yet another stage in their abuse.

THE MARRIAGE

There is still one boundary that not all abusive fathers cross. That is the boundary of full sexual intercourse with a daughter. The fathers who cross that boundary may use two very different rationales. For some the fear of pregnancy dictates that they have intercourse only with a pre-pubescent child. They stop having intercourse when their daughter reaches twelve or thirteen. That does not mean that the sexual abuse ends. It does mean that they retreat to other forms of abuse and, possibly, to other victims in the family. For others, the opposite occurs. Although they have broken every other rule in a father-child relationship, they do not begin intercourse until the girl reaches puberty. In their eyes, she is no longer a child at that point.

THE DIVORCE

The sexual abuse may be terminated in a variety of ways. One way is that the victim tells an adult what is happening. That person may be her mother or a mandated reporter. She keeps telling adults until someone reports the abuse to the authorities. Another way it ends is that the father is no longer in the home because of death or divorce. A third way is that the daughter leaves the home. She may leave for a variety of reasons: to go away to school, to live with another relative, to live on her own, to marry, or to run away from her father. Still another way is when the victim stands up to her father and tells him she will report him if he approaches her again. If the father accepts her decision, it is possible that he will continue to molest the other children in the family. The effects of the abuse are discussed in Chapter VI.

TRACY'S STORY

Tracy Miller is the eldest of four children. Her sister Sally is three years younger; her sister Nancy, five years younger; and her brother Douglas, seven years younger than Tracy. Tracy's father has his own insurance business; her mother works part time as a waitress at a local country club. Although she can't remember exactly when it started, Tracy first was sexually abused shortly after her brother's birth. She does remember that it started when she was in second grade. She remembers worrying that her teacher, Ms. Gates, might find out what she was doing.

Tracy's father had a small office in the city. Sometimes he had extra work to do and went to the office for a few hours on Sundays. He said he needed the peace and quiet of the office, rather than bringing work home. Soon after Douglas was born, Mr. Miller began going to work every Sunday. He asked Tracy to go along and be his "little secretary." She really enjoyed helping her dad. She felt grown-up and important. She was happy to be away from her new baby brother, who cried so much and required constant attention. Feeling like an only child for a few hours was a welcome treat.

At the office Tracy folded brochures, stuffed envelopes, and stamped them. Her folding was not always even, but Mr. Miller didn't seem to mind. Sometimes he gave her a small "salary" for her work; other times he took her to lunch at a nearby restaurant. The owner knew her father and always complimented him on his very attractive "date." Sundays became special to Tracy. She felt grown-up and proud of her father. Sally often asked to come along, but Mr. Miller insisted that she was too young. Tracy was pleased that she didn't have to share her day with anyone else.

One Sunday, while driving to the city, Mr. Miller pulled Tracy close to him in the car. He was talking about the chocolate sundaes they would have later when she felt his hand between her legs. She squirmed away from him. He kept driving, and nothing was said about the incident. A few weeks later it happened again. This time her dad told her that she was his special girl and what he was doing was a way of showing that he loved her in a very special way.

After that, every Sunday's drive became an opportunity for molestation. During the week her dad would take Tracy on errands, never taking the other children with them. Each time he would fondle her and tell her what a good girl she was. Tracy had many conflicting feelings about what was happening. She loved her dad and liked being the special child in the family. She enjoyed the money and presents that her dad gave her. She didn't want to lose those things. Tracy was also afraid—afraid that her father would be angry with her if she didn't cooperate with him. He had used his belt on her sisters, but never on Tracy. She didn't want to risk that punishment. At the same time, she was afraid that someone would find out what her father was doing. She wasn't sure what could happen if someone found out, but she thought it must be something bad because her dad kept warning her not to tell.

Tracy also was angry with her mother. Whenever she tried to get out of going with her father, her mother would always say, "You have to go. You're your dad's best helper. He depends on you." As time went by, Tracy was also mad at her mother for going back to work and for working nights. By age ten, Tracy was having oral sex with her father. Home was not a safe place anymore, since her father was in charge every weekday evening while her mother worked. Several times she asked her mother about getting a day job. Her mother said she needed the nights away from the family, and besides, Tracy and her dad made a fine baby-sitting team.

As the years went by Tracy felt more and more guilty. She was sure that everyone at school must know what was going on at her house. Her sexual experiences made her feel older than other girls her age. Many of them were just starting to date when, at thirteen, she was having intercourse with her father.

Tracy didn't fit in with other freshmen, nor did she really have much in common with the older group in high school. She was very lonely at school. Schoolwork was the farthest thing from her mind as her father made more and more demands on her. Her grades were poor, her friends nonexistent. Because her father kept a tight rein on her, she knew she'd never have a boyfriend. Mr. Miller would not let her baby-sit for anyone except her brother. When she had wanted to try out for the band, her father would not allow it. He said it was because of her grades, but Tracy knew that he didn't want her to be away from home for practices and football games. He had decreed that she could not date until her senior year. Until then there were to be no phone conversations with boys. When she protested, he said that it was his job to protect her from boys who would have wild ideas.

Finally, in desperation, she asked her mother to intervene on her behalf with her father. She wanted some changes in the strict rules that he had set down. Her mother refused to be an intermediary. She told Tracy that the rules were for her own good. Besides, what her husband said had always been law; she was not about to risk his anger.

In her sophomore year things were no better. When Tracy tried to avoid her father's advances, she was threatened with a variety of punishments: beatings, being grounded through high school, or being sent to a strict boarding school where the rules were even more confining than the ones at home. Tracy felt trapped and alone. She had no friends and no one to help her deal with this man who had become more a warden than a father.

Again Tracy turned to her mother. She had decided to tell her the whole story. Surely then her mother would make her father stop the abuse. She waited for a time to catch her mother alone, which was difficult because of the other children and her mother's work schedule. When Tracy tried to get the words out, she could hardly speak above a whisper. After she spoke there was a silence that seemed endless. Her mother said nothing. Tracy waited for the assurance she longed for. Eventually her mother began gathering her keys, purse, and uniform to get ready for work. She turned to the sobbing Tracy and said, "You must never speak of this again. Your father is sick, and there is nothing I can do about it. Try to keep away from him."

In some ways Tracy was not surprised by her mother's reaction. They had never been close. Tracy had resented having to do much of the work in the family. She felt that she had been more of a "mother" to her brother and sisters than had their own mother. She had hoped, however, that her mother would do something to end the abuse.

For the next few weeks she tried to do as her mother suggested, but she was unsuccessful in avoiding her father. During that time her mother went on as though nothing had been said. Tracy was furious with her mother for letting her down again.

Finally she went to see her school counselor and told her that her father was sexually abusing her. As a result of the report that was made, Tracy is living in a foster home, as are her brother and sisters. She no longer has to worry about her father bothering her. He has been arrested and ordered to stay away from his children. Her mother is very angry with Tracy and says that Tracy made up the whole story because she resented the family rules. A court date has been set for next month. Much will be decided at that time. In the meantime Tracy has mixed feelings about what has happened. She is relieved that she no longer has to worry about her father molesting her. At the same time she loves her father very much and misses him. They had many good times together when he was not being sexual with her. She doesn't miss her mother very often. She's angry with her for not helping her and feels betrayed. Mrs. Miller is standing by her husband. Allowing him to stay in the home meant that the children had to be placed in foster homes. Tracy's younger sister, Sally, has told her that Mr. Miller had been sexually abusing her as well for the past three years. She too is relieved that Tracy told someone and brought the abuse to an end.

Unfortunately the two younger children, Nancy and Douglas, are very angry with Tracy and refuse to have any contact with her. They blame her for breaking up the family and causing trouble for Mr. Miller.

Aftermath

Several elements might have been different in Tracy's story. If she hadn't told anyone, it is likely that the abuse would have continued for years, until she left home. It is also predictable that not only Sally but eventually Nancy would have been victimized. When there is more than one girl in the family, the other girls are at high risk for abuse.

If her mother had responded to Tracy's plea for help, the

current living arrangements might be quite different. To protect her daughter she might have insisted that her husband leave the house. The court would have assisted in this process. It is likely that, with the father out of the house and ordered not to contact his children, the four children would have remained in their home with their mother.

How this case is resolved would differ somewhat from state to state. The fact that his wife is siding with him, the fact that he has been a model citizen with no arrest record; the fact that he has been an active church member; and the fact that many people are willing to attest to his good character and work record are all advantages for Mr. Miller. He may not be convicted of the charges. If he is not, it is probable that all of the children will be returned to the home. It is also probable that if that occurs, none of the problems in the family will be resolved. The abuse will continue, although it is likely that Sally and Nancy will be victims, rather than Tracy. After all, Tracy has demonstrated that she won't keep the secret.

If Mr. Miller is convicted he may be sent to prison or he may be put on probation and required to receive counseling. The living arrangements for the children will depend partly upon whether Mr. Miller returns home. It is possible that Tracy will remain in the foster home and the other three children will be returned to Mrs. Miller. It is also possible that only Douglas will be returned, or that Mrs. Miller's protection of her husband will lead her to be judged an unfit mother. In that case, all the children could remain in foster homes for an indefinite time.

There is no ending for Tracy's story. It is clear that the problems going on in her family have been there for a long time. No judge's decision will be able to erase them.

OTHER PATTERNS

As indicated previously, father-daughter sexual abuse is the most prevalent pattern of sexually abusive behavior. Sometimes girls are victimized by more than one family member. Lucy was the victim of two of her teenage brothers as well as a male cousin. In a recent court case it was disclosed that a ten-year-old girl was molested by her father, three uncles, and her grandfather who was the father of the other four molesters!

Girls are also abused by female relatives, including mothers, sisters, aunts, cousins, and grandmothers. Girls who are victims of female abusers often report a pattern of extreme physical cruelty or ritualistic torture accompanying the sexual abuse. Females who abuse females are rarely reported, principally because the victims fear for their lives.

SUMMARY

"Tracy" is a composite of many women with whom I have spoken about their sexual abuse. If you are a victim of some of the same things that Tracy experienced, perhaps you see some differences in what has happened to you. Each sexual abuse case, like each person, is unique. However, the victim's pain, anger, confusion, and unearned sense of guilt seem to occur in all cases, regardless of the specific details.

DISCUSSION TOPICS

1. Imagine that Tracy is a classmate of yours. For some reason she decides to confide in you about the abuse. What would you say to her?

2. Even though she has told you her secret, she tells you not to let anyone else know about it. What would you do?

3. What is a foster home? What would be the advantages for Tracy in a foster home? Would there be disadvantages?

4. Write an ending for Tracy's story and compare it with those of your classmates.

5. Role-play Tracy and her mother as Tracy reveals her secret. Try it a second time with a different ending.

6. Find out how sexual abuse cases are handled in your area. Contact the agency responsible for investigating such cases.

7. Who is to blame for what happened to Tracy?

CHAPTER IV

Boys as Victims

The topic of males as victims of sexual abuse has received much less attention in books and articles than has that of females as victims. When boys are mentioned, it is more likely to be as a victim of a pedophile than as a victim of a family member. There are several reasons why information is so limited about boys who are sexually abused within the family. Let us consider these reasons individually.

1. Sexual abuse has been a major issue for feminist groups and the feminist press.

   The women's movement in the United States has succeeded in making people aware of the many injustices directed toward women in a male-dominated society. One of these injustices has been father-daughter incest. Feminist writers have made major contributions toward bringing this issue to the attention of all citizens. There has been no similar organized movement to speak for male victims. As a result there is less awareness that sexual abuse is a crime perpetrated against both sexes.

2. Support services for abused males are limited.

   Much of what has been written about sexual abuse has been based on information gathered from victims who come to rape crisis centers, women's support groups, or programs for sexually abused children. The typical victim who utilizes these services is female. Even groups available to adults who were molested as children are often sponsored by women's crisis centers, YWCAs, or other organizations identified with females. The male has fewer resources from which to seek help as an adolescent or as an adult.

3. Societal expectations for males interfere with reporting.

Boys are less likely than girls to tell anyone in authority that they have been abused. Some female sexual abuse is reported because the victim is pregnant or is afraid she will become pregnant. Neither is a motivating factor for boys to report abuse.

The infrequency with which boys report is related to other societal factors. Boys are raised with different social messages than those directed to girls. "Being a man" in many families means handling things alone. In such families asking for help is equated with being weak and less than a man.

Another message boys often receive is that showing certain feelings is not acceptable. It is masculine to show anger by punching someone or something, but it is not acceptable to let anyone know that a male is experiencing fear, confusion, or sadness. Such feelings must be kept concealed since they may detract from the "macho" image.

4. The concern about homosexuality perpetuates secrecy in males.

In addition to being trained not to ask for help and not to show their "unacceptable" feelings, boys are cautioned to avoid anything that may associate them with homosexuality. As young children they are steered away from playing with girls, showing interest in dolls, or playing "sissy" games. Before they reach adolescence boys are made aware of various colors, clothing styles, and interests that are designated gay or feminine and are to be avoided at all costs.

Boys are most likely to be abused by males. The male victim may be afraid that the abuse has made him a homosexual. He may worry that something he did or said implied that this was the case. The last thing he wants to do is call attention to this possibility, so he does not tell anyone about the molestation.

Boys are sexually victimized within the family. The general public is less likely to be aware of this victimization because of the preceding reasons. Boys do not report sexual abuse. Thus there is less opportunity to study or interview male victims. They do not receive help because they remain silent.

MALE VICTIMS AND PEDOPHILES

Boys are much more likely than girls to be molested by pedophiles. Thus, when we consider the estimate that one of seven boys will be sexually victimized, we must be aware that, unlike girls, as many as half of all male victims will be abused by strangers or casual acquaintances. This victimization is primarily related to one factor: availability. Parents tend to be less protective of boys than they are of girls. Boys are usually allowed to stay out later and roam farther from home than are girls of the same age. A walk through any video-game arcade or shopping mall in the evening hours will confirm this male freedom. The observer will see boys alone, boys in twos, boys in small groups but few girls. The pedophile will make his selection from the available "crop" that consists primarily of males.

Boys may be repeatedly molested by the same pedophile. They may be given money, gifts, drugs, or special privileges in return for silence. Others may be molested by a series of pedophiles because they are alone, available, and emotionally needy. Child molesters take full advantage of boys who are lonely and in need of affection. These boys are easily identified by the skilled pedophile in the course of a brief conversation. Harold, for instance, might approach a boy playing a video game. He would have spent some time observing him to make certain that he was alone. The dialogue might go as follows:

Harold: You're really good at this game.
Victim: The last couple of days, I haven't done so well. I hit 500 Saturday.
Harold: I'd sure like to be able to do that. How about if I pay for the next game and you give me some pointers?
Victim: It's your money.
(During the game and perhaps a couple of others that he would pay for, Harold would give the boy a great deal of praise and encouragement. After establishing some trust, he would continue with some crucial questions.)
Harold: It's getting pretty late. Are you heading home?
Victim: In a while. I'm in no hurry.
Harold: Well, your parents might be worrying about you.
Victim: Ha, that's a laugh.
Harold: What do you mean?

The response might be one of several that would inform Harold that this is a boy who doesn't receive much care.

The boy might say: "Nobody's home. My mom's out with her boyfriend," or, "They're too busy arguing to notice that I'm gone," or, "They're over at the tavern every night till it closes. They won't be worrying about me."

In this brief exchange Harold has learned several things about this boy. Based on the way he responds to praise, Harold knows that he does not receive much positive attention. Since he responds well to it, Harold will give him more to build trust. He also has found out that the boy frequents the arcade, so the odds are good that he'll be able to find him there again. Most important, he has learned that the boy has no supervision. His relationship with his parent or parents is poor. They will not be out looking for him if he is fifteen minutes late getting home.

Harold may build this relationship over several visits to the arcade before he attempts any molestation, or he may offer to drive the boy home, molest him, and then disappear in search of other victims. Either way, it is doubtful that the victim will tell his parents or anyone else about the attack. He would not expect anyone to care what happened to him, and he would not want to risk the possibility of having a curfew set for him, even for a few days.

FATHER-SON ABUSE

Within the family, male victims are most likely to be abused by their father. Father-son abuse is both similar to and different from father-daughter abuse. It is similar in that it involves the use of power and coercion in which a parent takes advantage of the parental role to misuse a child. As in father-daughter abuse, the father is likely to abuse more than one child in the family. Other sons are at risk, as are daughters. Because pregnancy is not an issue, the age of twelve or thirteen is not as crucial in father-son abuse as it is with daughters.

Father-son abuse is more likely to be accompanied by physical abuse than is father-daughter abuse. Thus the male victim may have a more openly hostile and violent relationship with his father than a female victim would have. If the abuse of the male is revealed, outsiders are likely to be surprised about the sexual component but well aware of the negative father-son relationship. Such comments as, "There always was bad blood between them," or "Everybody knew he hated his father," are typical responses to father-son abuse. This is in sharp contrast to the impression of outsiders when father-daughter sexual abuse is reported. Comments such as, "They always seemed like such a happy family," or, "He's always been such a good family man," are indicative of the less violent nature of father-daughter sexual abuse. Some fathers are both physically and sexually abusive toward their daughters. These are the minority, however, as threat of physical harm is the more common pattern.

Stages

Some father-son sexual abuse situations follow the pattern described in Chapter III. The son may be two or three when the father begins to give him special attention. Gradually the sexual component is introduced into the relationship, and the engagement, marriage, and divorce stages follow.

Because of the physical abuse that is often a part of father-son sexual abuse, it is believed that the stage-by-stage escalation of the abuse is not the predominant pattern. In the more common pattern, the encounter period and part of the engagement period are omitted. There seems to be less concern by the abusive father to rationalize or justify abuse to a male child than to a female child. This may be related to societal messages that boys are supposed to be strong and handle anything that comes their way.

Like sexual abuse of females, there is no one pattern that fits all father-son abuse. In some instances sexual activity may be limited to genital fondling. In others the abusive behavior may be mutual masturbation, oral sex, sodomy, or a combination of activities.

Reactions

The victims share many of the reactions that females have to sexual abuse. They are confused, frightened, angry, and humiliated. They feel trapped and without hope of being rescued from the abuse. In addition, boys may experience doubts about their masculinity and fear that they are homosexual because they have been victimized by someone of the same sex. It is essential for every child, male or female, who is sexually abused to realize that nothing he or she said or did brought on the abuse. It is the adult abuser who is totally responsible for the misuse of the child.

JIMMY'S STORY

Jimmy was twelve when he ran away from home the first time. He didn't get far. He was picked up by the police while trying to hitchhike to his grandmother's house. He was brought back with a warning to stay close to home. The next time he ran away, he managed to stay away for a week, sleeping in friends' basements and hiding from their parents as well as his own. When the mother of one of his

friends discovered him, she called his father to come and
get him. His father beat him with his belt and told him it
was only a sample of what would happen if he tried that
again.

At thirteen Jimmy did try again and was picked up by
the local youth officer. For the first time, someone took the
time to listen to him, rather than lecturing him about being
a runaway. What the youth officer heard was an all too
familiar story of a boy running from a sexually and physically abusive father.

Jimmy is the eldest of three brothers. As long as he can
remember, the whole family has been afraid of his father.
He learned very early not to cross his father, not to argue
with him nor to expect help if his father blamed him for
any real or imagined offense. The first sexual advance he
remembers from his father was when he was three and his
mother was in the hospital giving birth to his second
brother. Genital fondling became a nightly ritual as his
father came in at night to "check on" Jimmy. Over the next
ten years there had been more and more frequent episodes
of physical and sexual abuse.

Jimmy describes his father as always angry and ready to
explode. On several occasions he has witnessed his father
engaging in sexual activity with his younger brothers.
When he has attempted to intervene, his father has beaten
him unmercifully. He has developed several plans for kill-
ing his father and talks about how much better off the
whole family would be if his father were dead. These
thoughts both please and frighten Jimmy. He has con-
cluded that running away is the only strategy that will both
stop the abuse and keep him from going to prison on a
homicide charge.

The youth officer assures Jimmy that by telling his story

he has taken a major step in protecting himself and his brothers from further harm. Together with the state's child protection agency, the youth officer will work to see that Jimmy and his brothers have a safe and healthy environment away from their abusive father.

OTHER PATTERNS

Jimmy was abused by his real father. His abuser could have also been a stepfather, cousin, or other male relative. He might have been victimized by several men in his family. He might also have been sexually abused by his mother.

Like mother-daughter incest, little has been written about mother-son incest. One major difference between the two is that in mother-daughter sexual abuse the father or father figure usually lives in the home. In mother-son abuse it is more likely that no father or father figure is in the home. The son, regardless of how young he may be, is treated as the "man of the house" by his mother. She may justify having her son share her bed on the grounds of her loneliness and need for comfort. As in all forms of sexual abuse, the needs of the child are not taken into account. Only the needs of the abuser are given any consideration. The boy who is trapped in a sexual relationship with his mother experiences confusion about his own sexual identity as well as the roles of parents and children.

Although all sexual abuse is damaging and can result in long-term psychological effects, experts believe that in cases where the mother is the abuser the emotional damage to both male and female victims is especially devastating. In Chapter VI we consider the effects of sexual abuse in detail.

SUMMARY

Boys are most likely to be sexually abused by other males, either strangers or family members. When the abuse is at the hands of family members, it is likely that physical abuse is also directed toward the victim. Reactions to the abuse are similar for boys and girls. However, boys tend to have greater anger toward their father than do girls. This may be related to the presence of physical abuse in father-son incest. Boys may be victimized by their mother or other female relatives. This seems to result in even greater psychological trauma than abuse by male relatives.

DISCUSSION TOPICS

1. We have considered some societal expectations that prevent boys from reporting sexual abuse. What are some others? How are they different from the messages that girls receive?
2. What resources are available for sexually abused boys in your area? in your school? Find out and report to your class.
3. What can be done to protect children from pedophiles?
4. Discuss the reasons that boys are reluctant to report sexual abuse. How can this reluctance be changed?
5. If Jimmy had been "successful" in running away, what would happen to him? How would his life be different?
6. Invite someone who works in a shelter or other program for runaways to talk with your class about their services and the children who require them.
7. Consider some reasons for the particularly negative effects of mother-child sexual abuse.

CHAPTER V

The Family

Sexual abuse takes place in the context of the family. As you are aware, the composition of families varies greatly. Some consist of one parent and a child; others of two parents and a child or children. Many children grow up in "single-parent" homes in which one parent, usually the father, does not live in the home because of divorce, death, or some other circumstance. A single-parent home may have other adults in residence, including the parent's boyfriend or girlfriend, a grandparent, or some other relative who takes an active part in family decisions.

The term "blended family" has been used to describe a family in which both the husband and wife bring children from previous marriages together to form a new family. The children become stepbrothers and stepsisters to one another. They each acquire either a stepmother or a stepfather. Sometimes this "blend" is full time; other times it occurs only on weekends.

Some children have a large extended family; that is, they have many aunts, uncles, grandparents, or cousins. Extended family members usually do not live with the child's immediate family, but they have access to the home and may visit frequently if they live in the area.

It used to be that if someone were describing the typical American family it would be a two parent/two child grouping. When you think of your own family and the

families of your friends and classmates, that image probably does not fit.

Child sexual abuse takes place in all styles of families. A
characteristic that all such families share is that they are
multiproblem families. Sexual abuse is one of the problems, but not the only problem present in the family. Let us
consider some of the other problems that may be present in
a family with sexual abuse problems.

1. *Marital problems*

If both parents live in the home, it is almost always the
case that the marital relationship is poor. Perhaps the parents have had trial separations or talked about a divorce.
In some instances there has been an emotional and physical
divorce without a legal agreement. The parents may be
staying together because they cannot afford a divorce or
because of other circumstances that make a divorce seem-
ingly impossible.

The marital problems may not be apparent to people
outside of the family. The parents may work very hard to
project to the community an image of a united family. In
reality they may have little positive communication with
each other. At one extreme this may mean that the children
live in a home where the adults are constantly arguing and
criticizing each other. At the other extreme there may be so
little verbal communication between the parents that the
children never know what to expect. Either extreme creates
a very tense environment for the children, who must try to
make some sense out of the confusion.

2. *Health problems*

When a family member is in poor health for a prolonged
period of time, a great deal of stress is created in the family.

In sexual abuse cases it is not uncommon that the abuse began at a time when the mother was ill. She may have been hospitalized for weeks or even months. During her absence the children would have had to take on additional responsibilities. The eldest daughter might find herself in a "little mother" role, taking care of younger siblings as well as managing household responsibilities. The following example is all too typical.

Sara was the eldest of three daughters. For as long as she could remember, her mother had been "ailing" with heart problems. Although she was only in first grade, Sara helped with the cooking, cleaning, laundry, and care of her two sisters. Her mother was hospitalized frequently. When she was at home she had to spend most of her time in bed, so Sara's responsibilities actually increased when her mother was released. Because her father was a farmer who had to be away from home all day, Sara had to make certain that her mother took her medicine and stayed in bed.

The summer before Sara started second grade, her mother was away for her longest hospital stay. It was at this time that Sara's father began molesting her. With her mother gone and no close neighbors, Sara was defenseless. She prayed every night that her mother would come home and make her father stop molesting her. When her mother did come home, the abuse continued. Sara was afraid to tell her mother what was going on for fear she would make her sick again and be responsible for sending her back to the hospital.

In situations like Sara's, several factors are predictable. The father will use the mother's health as a threat to his victim or victims. Sara's father often warned her that telling about the abuse would result in her mother's death. The eldest child still at home is most likely to be given the role of "little mother." The family roles are reversed, with the children having to take care of the parents rather than the other way around. Sara learned early that her mother could not take care of her or protect her. Instead she was expected to be her mother's caretaker and protector. Even if her mother had completely recovered, it is doubtful that Sara would have told her what was happening. Both of her parents had taught her that children's needs did not have the same priority as adult needs.

3. *Alcohol/drug problems*

As mentioned in Chapter II, some people who molest their children or allow them to be molested by others have alcohol or drug problems. In the majority of sexual abuse cases, drugs or alcohol are not contributing factors. If drug or alcohol problems do exist, they exist as problems separate from the sexual abuse. That is, sexual abuse is not caused by alcohol or drug abuse. Most people who abuse their children are not alcoholics or drug addicts. Most people who are alcoholics or drug abusers are not child molesters.

When sexual abuse is discovered in a family, it is common for the molester to claim that he was drunk or high on drugs. That is simply a way of saying, "I'm not responsible for the sexual abuse of my child. It was the liquor or drugs that made me do this terrible thing. I'm not that kind of person."

If caught, he will volunteer to enter a rehabilitation program to cure his addiction. Although this is a transparent attempt to avoid serving time in prison, it has been relatively successful with judges and juries. Most people want to believe that no one would consciously, willingly molest their own children.

In homes where alcoholism or drug abuse is combined with sexual abuse, it is likely that the children will suffer physical neglect. They may lack sufficient food, clothing, housing, or other basic needs. That is because such addictions are costly and often interfere with the addicted parent's ability to work and provide for the family. Neglected children have a high likelihood of being reported to the state agency that protects children. The authorities may learn of the sexual abuse after the children have been removed from an environment of neglect. Such cases represent a small percentage of sexual abuse cases.

4. *Financial problems*

Most families experience financial difficulties on occasion, with the result that a wanted item cannot be purchased or a vacation has to be postponed. In contrast, financial problems may be more constant and produce more stress in the family. They may occur at any income level, as illustrated in the following example.

Mr. and Mrs. Davis wanted a home in the suburbs. They both were willing to work hard to get it. Mr. Davis has a full-time job with an insurance company. On Saturdays and several evenings a week he clerks in a men's clothing store. Mrs. Davis is a receptionist in the emergency room of the local hospital. She works from 11:00 p.m. to 7:00 a.m. four nights a week. After they bought their dream house, the Davises had planned that she would stop working. However, the mortgage payments and ever increasing property taxes have prevented this from happening. Mr. Davis's commissions are down. They are finding it difficult to do much more than meet their monthly home obligations.

They have very little furniture in their new home and little hope that they will be able to buy more for some time.

They have no savings and worry about what they would do
if their home needed any repairs. Money and the lack of it
are constant topics in the home. Although the Davises have
the home they dreamed about, their work schedule prevents them from enjoying it. The little time they have
together is spent arguing and worrying about money.
Instead of bringing them happiness, their dream home has
made their lives a nightmare.

Certainly, sexual abuse does not occur in every family
that has financial problems. In some instances, however,
the man who loses his job or cannot support his family as
he thinks he should feels that he has failed as a man and as
a husband. He is aware of his wife's disappointment in his
inability to be the provider she thought he was. He may
turn to his children for reassurance and nurturance. In a
sexual abuse situation he can feel in control of something
in his family.

5. *Interpersonal problems*

An effective way that many people deal with stress in
their lives is to share their worries with friends or extended
family members. Sometimes just talking about a problem
with a concerned person will help clarify issues and possible solutions. Just getting things "out on the table" can
provide some relief from the stress. Adults who abuse their
children may not have the kind of relationship with others
that makes this kind of sharing possible. Instead of being
able to reach outside the immediate family for help, they
are more inclined to believe that problems in the family
must be kept secret. Talking things over with "outsiders"
would be considered a betrayal of the family. These attitudes result in a lack of trust of others and a guardedness
around anyone who is not part of the immediate family.
The adults in the family may have many acquaintances, but
few if any close friends or confidants.

With this strong feeling of mistrust and the importance of family secrecy, it is unlikely that sexually abusive adults will voluntarily seek help from strangers in counseling or family service agencies. Usually they find themselves in counselor's offices only after the abuse has been reported and the court has ordered the family members to use counseling services. The years of living in a household with many family secrets result in a predictable reluctance to be honest and open in a counseling session. It may take weeks or months before family members begin to acknowledge that there are problems in the family.

6. *Mental illness or retardation*
Although most people who sexually abuse their children are not mentally ill, mental illness or retardation are sometimes factors in the family. The combination of mental illness and sexual abuse occurs in several ways. The abuser may be mentally ill and not in control of himself or herself. Another possibility is that the nonabusing spouse is mentally ill or retarded and cannot protect the molested child; the abuser takes advantage of the other parent's condition in abusing the children. Although rare, sexual abuse cases have been reported in which both parents were mentally ill and had no understanding of parental roles. It is also possible that the victim may be mentally ill or retarded, which makes the child especially vulnerable. If the child is able to communicate effectively, he or she is not likely to be believed. If the child has difficulty communicating, the abuser does not have to worry about being reported.

7. *Violence in the family*
The sexually abused child may live in a violent home. If the father physically abuses his wife, her fear of him may keep her from protecting her children from sexual abuse.

The violence directed toward their mother is a clear message to the children that if they do not comply with the father's every wish, the same violence may be meted out to them. Sometimes that message is made even stronger as the father physically abuses some of the children. Usually the sexually abused child is not also physically abused. However, in the presence of violence directed toward others in the family, the child understands what could happen if the father's demands are not met.

The preceding problems are some of the factors that may be present in a sexually abusive family. They may occur in any combination. As previously stated, sexual abuse is a symptom of a family in crisis. The problems that are components of that crisis vary from family to family. All of the problems have to be dealt with for the family to function effectively and for the sexual abuse to end.

FAMILY PATTERNS

Sexual abuse is most likely to occur in families that exhibit one of four patterns. Let us take a closer look at sexually abusive families.

The Absent Spouse

In families where the mother or father does not live with the children because of death, separation, or divorce, the children are often given additional responsibilities to make up for the absent parent. If the mother is not in the home, the children, especially the daughters, may have homemaking and child-rearing responsibilities. In sexual abuse situations the father expects his daughter or daughters to substitute for his absent wife in every way, including the role of sex partner.

In instances when the father is absent, some mothers turn to their children for nurturance and sexual gratification. They are particularly inclined to turn to their male children for such attention. Derek's mother did exactly that.

Derek was two years old when his parents were divorced. His father moved to another state and made no attempt to see him or contact him; he has since remarried and has two other children. Derek has seen his father twice at family gatherings. Both meetings were brief and uncomfortable. Derek's mother was very lonely after the divorce. She had few friends and no relatives in the suburb where she lived. Her job with a computer firm was very demanding. Her life centered on her job and Derek. Occasionally someone would ask her out or attempt to arrange a blind date, but she always declined. Her marriage had been unhappy, and she had no interest in getting into a relationship with a man again.

Shortly after Derek's father left, his mother began taking Derek into her bed at night. It eased her loneliness to have him beside her. This became a nightly pattern. By the time he was three Derek was being fondled by his mother. Sexual activities escalated to oral sex. Derek was confused and frightened by his mother's attention. He felt trapped and alone.

When he reached school age Derek felt relieved to be away from his mother, even for a short time. As he got older, Derek joined the Cub Scouts. Soon afterward, his mother rearranged her work schedule so she could be his den mother. She is also Derek's Sunday School teacher and the treasurer of his Little League baseball team. Derek's teachers and the parents of his friends admire his mother for her participation in his activities. Only Derek knows of their sexual relationship. Lately he has been having nightmares and has reverted to bedwetting. His school work has been declining, and his behavior has become babyish. When the principal suggested the services of the school counselor, Derek's mother was irate. She promised to tutor him at home. Derek is thinking about calling his father and asking if he can move in with him.

Sometimes it is the noncustodial parent who sexually abuses the children when they visit. In this situation the abuse may be a way of getting back at the custodial parent. It should be noted that the number of single-parent homes is increasing. The vast majority of single parents do not molest their children.

Dependent Husband/Domineering Wife

A second family pattern that is observed in child sexual abuse cases is that of a wife who is in charge of the family and a husband who is in charge of nothing. Although they may be the same age, the domineering wife complains that her husband is like an additional child requiring her care. The dependent husband leaves all decisions and choices to his wife. He seeks affection from her but is not successful in getting it. He feels inadequate and angry with his wife but would not dare challenge her authority. In his anger and his loneliness he turns to a female who is less threatening: His daughter is more accepting of him than is his wife. Henry is an example of a dependent husband.

Henry married Clare against her family's wishes. Clare came from a middle-class family that looked down on Henry. In their eyes he came from an impoverished family and had nothing to offer Clare. They had hoped that their daughter would marry a professional man, perhaps a lawyer. When Clare met Henry, he was a bank guard and she was an office manager at the bank. Clare liked going out with Henry. He always agreed with her suggestions about where to go, he was easy to get along with, and there were none of the arguments that Clare had encountered with her previous boyfriend. Henry was happy to have someone who would make the decisions about where to go and what to do.

The very things that they appreciated in each other when they dated became sources of anger and unhappiness in their marriage. Henry felt inferior to Clare. He could not compete with her verbally or in his career. Over the years she had had several promotions; he was in the same job he had when they were dating. He came to resent her take-charge manner and the fact that she never asked his opinion. Henry was angry with himself for not speaking up and for avoiding any conflict.

Clare often worked late hours at the bank while Henry baby-sat for their two daughters. He enjoyed being alone with his children. His wife was not there to pressure him about things that needed to be done around the house. He and his daughters played games, and for once he was the boss. Looking back, Henry is not certain how old his daughters were when the games he directed took on a sexual component. Neither of the girls had reached kindergarten age when he transformed hide-and-seek and peek-a-boo into opportunities to fondle and be fondled by his daughters. He does remember that he and his wife were no longer having sexual relations when the sexual abuse began.

When asked later by a police officer why he had turned to his children rather than an adult for sexual gratification, Henry was aghast. The thought of dating another woman while married was something he had never considered. He would not risk Clare's wrath nor the possibility that his marriage might be threatened by an extramarital affair. Besides, he was much more comfortable with his daughters than he would have been with another adult. Henry had convinced himself that molesting his daughters was less harmful than risking a dissolution of his unhappy marriage.

Possessive Husband/Passive Wife

In this family the husband controls everything. He decides how the money will be spent, where the family will go on vacations, who will be invited into *his* home, and everything else of any importance in the family. His family members are his possessions. In his eyes, the family exists to meet his needs. Although he is often considered a model citizen outside his home, he is a tyrant within it. He can be violent to his wife or his children. To avoid crossing him, his wife and children make certain that everything is done according to his wishes.

The passive wife in this family accepts her husband's direction in every way. She has very low self-esteem and believes that everything she is and has is attributable to her husband. She knows that she could never manage without him. It is possible that she was either physically or sexually abused as a child. She learned at that time that she was worth very little. Now she has married a man who confirms her ineptitude. Holding on to her marriage is more important to her than anything else in life. Because she probably does not work and may not even be able to drive a car, the passive wife is totally dependent on her husband.

Although the possessive husband may have enjoyed his

role of king in the early years of his marriage, eventually he becomes angry and disgusted with a wife who clings to him for everything. He considers his daughters to be more like adults than their mother is. Since, like their mother, they are his possessions, he feels that it is his right to do whatever he chooses to them. When he engages in sexual activity with one of his daughters, he rationalizes his behavior by saying that he is teaching her. He considers that his right as a father. Al is such a father.

Al is a respected lawyer in a small town. He serves on the school board and is a deacon in his church. His success is attested to by the large home he has provided for his wife, Helen, and their daughter, Tina. Helen and Al were high school sweethearts. They married before Al started law school. Helen did secretarial work at the college to support her husband until he graduated. When he opened his law office, Helen "retired." A year later Tina was born. Helen devotes her time to raising her daughter, caring for her home, and gardening. She describes Al as the social member of the family, while she is content to be at home. When Al has to go to meetings or receptions, he often takes Tina as his "date." Tina enjoys substituting for her mother and being the only nine-year-old at these adult activities.

In the ten years of their marriage, Al's and Helen's lives have gone in different directions. Professionally and socially, Al has excelled. Helen, always shy and content to stand in her husband's shadow, is unwilling to spend time away from her home. She complains of many aches and pains and insists that she is not well. Sending her daughter as her replacement at community events relieves Helen of a burdensome task.

Lately Al has become more impatient with his wife. He finds something to criticize whenever he comes home.

Helen avoids his tirades by going to bed early with a headache or some other malady. Tina prepares her father's dinner, and the two of them are often alone in the basement family room. When Al began fondling Tina, she was frightened, but she had learned never to question anything that her father did. Although Al was very gentle with her, Tina knew that he could become angry at any moment. He has told her that he is showing her how much he loves her and preparing her to be an adult.

Dependent Husband/Dependent Wife

Sometimes two adults who have difficulty managing their lives on their own find each other and marry. They marry to be taken care of by a spouse. Since they are not skilled at taking care of themselves, they are not able to meet the needs of their spouse. They look to their children to meet their needs. Stan and Sue are typical of such a dependency relationship.

Sue's father sexually abused her from the time she was four years old. She left home as soon as she finished high school. Getting away from her family was her major motivation for joining the Army. Sue and her mother were not close, and she told the recruiter that she hoped to be stationed as far away from her family as possible.

In the Army Sue was trained to program computers. When her enlistment period was up she left the military. Although she appreciated the training she had received, Sue had no regrets about leaving. Just as in school, she had made no close friends in the military. She always felt older and different from girls her own age. She preferred to stay to herself while others socialized.

Stan lived in the apartment across from Sue's. He taught

in a nearby school and came home from work at the same time Sue did. Conversations in the hallway led to shared dinners. Within a short time they were spending every evening together. Both Stan and Sue were loners, with no friends and no family ties. Stan's father had been an alcoholic who had physically abused all of the family members. When Stan's mother died he left home and had not been in contact with his father in many years.

Stan and Sue decided to marry after only a few months. They both saw marriage as the answer to their loneliness. What they could get from the marriage was of more importance than what they could give to each other. Although they never spoke of it, the loneliness did not disappear after the wedding. Sharing an apartment did not make trusting and communicating any easier. Lacking experience at being a friend, neither Stan nor Sue was capable of recognizing the signs that indicated a need for support or care from the other. They had learned nothing about being a spouse or a parent from their own parents.

Having children was a way for them to be loved and appreciated by other human beings. They looked to their children to meet their needs. Children were expected to be the caretakers of their parents. Stan began molesting his daughter when she was less than a year old. He felt that he was finally loved and important to someone.

Overall Characteristics

All of these two-parent families have some common characteristics. The most common in a sexually abusive family is that the marital relationship is poor. Often the couple are no longer having sexual relations when the molestation begins. If they are still having sexual relations, neither spouse considers their lovemaking satisfactory.

Sexually abusive parents may be repeating the pattern of their own childhood. The mother who was molested is inclined to marry a man who will molest her own children. The father who was molested will identify with his attacker. He chooses to become the attacker of his own children and experience the power that such abuse can provide for him.

Sex is not likely to be discussed in the sexually abusive family. The parents may have insufficient or inaccurate information about sex, which they perpetuate in their family. Confusion about human sexuality may be an issue for all members of the family.

Discussion of any substantive topic is rare. Opinions are not valued, nor are ideas from children accepted in this tightly structured family.

Because of the secrecy involved in sexual abuse, there is often an atmosphere of tension in the home. Something is going on in the family that no one wants to ask about or know about. There is often an awareness that if the wrong word or phrase is used, something will happen that will damage the family reputation.

SUMMARY

Most of the families in which sexual abuse takes place appear to be no different from any other family to the outsider. The parents seem to be model citizens in many ways. However, there are major differences between them and nonabusive families. Abusive parents believe that children are there to serve their needs. They deal with stress not by turning to other adults for help, but by turning to their children for comfort, revenge, and sexual gratification.

DISCUSSION TOPICS

1. Role-play Derek calling his father and asking if he can move in with him. Try several responses to Derek.
2. What do you think will happen to Tina? to her mother? to her father?
3. Sometimes sexual abusers state that they have fallen in love with their victim. How would you reply to that claim?
4. Respond to this statement: "Sexual abuse is not as bad as physical abuse. After all, nobody dies from being sexually abused."
5. In what ways are sexually abusive families different from your ideas of a "normal" family? In what ways are they the same?
6. How do we learn family roles? What ideas do you have to help sexually abused children learn other roles?
7. Which of the family problems common to sexually abusive families do you consider the most difficult to resolve? Why?

CHAPTER VI

The Effects of Sexual Abuse

From what you have already read, you probably have some ideas about the effects of sexual abuse on victims. Most of these effects are not as visible as the bruises and burns that result from physical abuse. In this chapter we shall look at many possible effects of sexual abuse. Not every survivor of abuse experiences all of these effects, nor are they necessarily evident at the time the abuse is occurring.

Physical Effects

Some physical effects of sexual abuse make it likely that the abuse will be discovered. The first of these is pregnancy. No accurate figures are available on the number of girls who become pregnant as a result of sexual abuse. Girls as young as ten and eleven have been impregnated by fathers, uncles, brothers, or cousins. Pregnancy of a minor brings questions that are likely to result in the arrest of the man responsible. The effect of the pregnancy on the victim is extremely traumatic.

Sexual abuse is sometimes discovered because the victim contracts a venereal disease. Venereal diseases can cause painful infections that can damage reproductive organs. The presence of a venereal disease in a child is a clear indication that sexual abuse has occurred. Other genital infections or discharges in the genital area may indicate sexual abuse. Lesions or swelling in the genital area may make it difficult for a victim to sit comfortably. Physical effects of sexual abuse are apparent in only a small minority of cases. For the most part sexually abused children suffer the effects quietly, without any observable clues that abuse is a component of their lives.

Emotional Effects

The emotional effects of sexual abuse can be devastating, not only to children, but also to adults who were molested as children. As each potential effect is considered, it is important to realize that not every victim experiences the same effects to the same degree. Each victim, each perpetrator, each situation is unique. Research indicates that most victims of sexual abuse experience many emotional effects, but some of the effects may not appear until adulthood. Counselors and support groups are available to help survivors deal with these effects whenever they occur.

1. *The loss of childhood.* Children who are abused sexually have been introduced to the adult world of sexuality. Whether they are three or thirteen when they are first molested, the result is that they feel older than their peers. Although they look like other children, inside they feel different and separate from others who worry about what to wear to school tomorrow. Victims of sexual abuse are worrying about whether "it" will happen again tonight and may have trouble fitting in with other children.

2. *Guilt.* Children who are abused often feel that they are somehow responsible for the abuse. As they

grow older they sometimes believe that they could have stopped the abuser or that they said or did something to encourage the abuse. They feel that they are bad because of what they were forced to do. The truth is that children do not control adults. Nothing that a child says or does or wears causes him or her to be abused. As was pointed out in the discussion of the family, the child is incidental in sexual abuse. The *adult's* problems lead to abuse. The child is a victim and is no more responsible than is the victim of a hit-and-run driver.

3. *Low self-esteem.* Because sexual abuse involves sexual activity that children eventually realize is inappropriate, victims often feel that they are bad. They wrongly believe that they are not as good as their peers or as deserving of praise or recognition. If something good happens to them or someone acknowledges their accomplishments, victims are inclined to believe that they do not deserve the recognition. Adolescents in particular seek negative attention by being truant, running away, being promiscuous, or misusing drugs and alcohol. When they get in trouble, authority figures confirm their "badness."

4. *Fear.* Many kinds of fear are associated with sexual abuse. Some victims have a constant fear of physical harm. The abuser may threaten the child with physical harm for not complying with his wishes. For others the threat may be unspoken, but the fact that others in the family are physically abused serves as a warning of what could happen to an uncooperative victim.

Separate from concerns about physical harm are

the fears of what would happen if the sexual abuse were discovered. The abuser may tell the child that if anyone finds out about what has been going on, the child will be put in jail or in a detention center or taken away from the family. There may also be threats about other family members: "Your mother will have a heart attack," or, "You'll all go on welfare," or, "All of you kids will go to an orphanage," are comments used by the abuser to keep a child from telling anyone about the abuse. These are very real possibilities to children, who are terrified that they might be responsible for the death of a parent or the dissolution of the family.

Victims of sexual abuse may be in a constant state of fear and anxiety about the next incident of molestation. They may lie awake at night waiting and wondering if something is going to happen. They may have nightmares about the abuse, and as adults they may continue to have fears about sleeping in a particular room or with the light off. Many adults who were molested as children have severe insomnia.

5. *Confusion.* The popular image of an adult, particularly a parent, is of one who would only want a child to do good things. When a child is molested, he or she feels real confusion about right and wrong. The child may sense that what is going on is wrong but cannot accept the possibility that Dad or Grandpa would ever do wrong. The confusion about right and wrong may cause the child to doubt his or her own judgment. Instead of concluding that the abuser is doing wrong, the child often concludes that there must be something wrong with him or her

for feeling uneasy or frightened by the abuse. This confusion and lack of confidence in being able to assess a situation can carry into adulthood. Adult women who were abused as children report that they continue to get talked into sexual situations with men because they're not certain of their own judgment.

6. *Depression.* Children who are abused carry a heavy emotional burden. They may feel alienated from their brothers and sisters and peers. They are carrying a secret that they are not supposed to share. The adults on whom they should be able to depend have let them down. The loneliness and guilt associated with sexual abuse may seem overwhelming. Depression may be linked to suicide attempts, drug and alcohol abuse, running away, and self-abusive behavior. Eating disorders like anorexia nervosa and bulimia have been linked with the depression resulting from sexual victimization.

7. *Anger.* It is a normal reaction to become angry when someone mistreats us. If they continue to mistreat us, we become more angry. Victims of sexual abuse are mistreated over a long period of time. They may be angry with themselves for not being able to escape the abuse. They may be angry with their father or another abuser who took advantage of their childhood. They are often especially angry with their mother who didn't notice what was happening or who didn't believe them when they tried to talk about the abuse.

Because victims are not allowed to release their anger in the family environment, they may keep it inside for years. As adults they may experience fre-

quent headaches, ulcers, or colitis and never associate these symptoms with the bottled-up rage that
has resulted from years of abuse.

8. *Inability to trust others.* Sexual abuse represents a
betrayal of trust. The person who was most trusted
by the child has betrayed that trust. As an adult, the
victim may find it difficult to trust anyone, especially those of the same sex as the perpetrator.
Sometimes women who were molested by a male
turn away from all men and seek homosexual relationships. Some adult women are so confused by
issues of trust that they repeatedly ally themselves
with men who deserve neither their trust nor their
companionship.

9. *Helplessness.* A victim of sexual abuse feels powerless against the abuser. The abuser is in charge and
controls the victim. A child or adolescent feels
defenseless when the abuser makes demands. This
vulnerability and helplessness may be noticed by
others. It is not unusual for the victim of sexual
abuse to be victimized by others in the family or the
neighborhood. Vicki was molested by her father,
her two elder brothers, her brother's friends, and
her best friend's father. She said nothing to anyone
about this abuse. As an adult she was raped by three
men whom she had dated. Still she said nothing.
Vicki believed that all men were like the ones who
had abused her. She thought that her experiences
were similar to those of most women. In a support
group she learned that this was not the case; she had
been trained to be a victim. Her participation in the
group is helping her to unlearn this victim role.

10. *Attitudes toward sexuality.* Adult sexuality involves

mutual sharing, concern for the needs of both partners, and an atmosphere of respect and trust. All of these factors are absent when an adult engages in sexual activity with a minor. No matter how gentle the abuser may appear, there is no question that he is in charge. The most basic need of a child to be treated as a child is violated. Only the needs of the adult are considered in sexual abuse. Premature sexual activity has lasting effects on the victim. The victim may feel like "damaged goods," that is, feel unworthy of relationships with members of the opposite sex. Many victims teach themselves to turn off all feelings while they are being molested. As adults they may continue to deny themselves any sexual feelings. They may react negatively when touched, especially if touched in a way that they were touched while being abused. These reactions may result in a poor sexual relationship within a marriage. The husband may become impatient with his wife's lack of interest. The wife often does not associate her adult avoidance of sexual contact with what happened to her as a child.

SUMMARY

The effects of sexual abuse vary from victim to victim. We cannot predict how any one person will be affected by abuse, nor can we predict the duration of those effects in adulthood. What is clear is that the longer sexual abuse goes on, the more likely it is that the victim will need professional help to overcome the effects. Support groups composed of other victims seem to be especially helpful to adult victims. Such groups are often sponsored by local mental health agencies, YWCAs, battered women's organizations, and college counseling centers.

Help for children and adolescents is available through schools, churches, and agencies.

DISCUSSION TOPICS

1. How would you help a friend who exhibited some of the effects of sexual abuse?
2. Identify resources in your community for victims of sexual abuse. How could you help someone "connect" with the best resource?
3. Ask someone who works with people with eating disorders to speak to your class. What connections do they make between eating disorders and sexual abuse?
4. Discuss the concept of learned helplessness. How might it influence the victim's adult life?
5. Some people believe that children born of an incestuous relationship are retarded. Research this topic and report your findings to the class.
6. Several kinds of fear were mentioned regarding abuse. What other fears may be related to a history of sexual abuse?
7. Low self-esteem presents many problems for children and adolescents. How can peers or teachers raise someone's self-esteem?

CHAPTER VII

Treatment for Sexual Abuse Victims

In Chapter VI we considered some of the possible effects of sexual abuse on victims. If you are presently being sexually abused or if sexual abuse has been a past experience, it is important that you participate in a program specifically designed for survivors of abuse. Most treatment programs offer services to all family members. Our emphasis in this chapter is on the treatment of child and adolescent victims, rather than on other family members.

MEDICAL SERVICES

As a victim of sexual abuse, your body has been used without your permission. Regardless of the specific nature of the abuse, regardless of how recently or how long ago the abuse took place, many victims worry that their body has been permanently injured by the abuse. Although that is rarely the case, only a complete medical examination by a physician who understands the nature of sexual abuse can eliminate the fear. Follow-up medical services are required if pregnancy or venereal disease has resulted from the abuse.

SEX EDUCATION

Contradictory as it may seem, victims of sexual abuse often come from homes where sexuality has never been discussed. Though introduced prematurely to sexual activity, many victims have limited understanding and inaccurate information about human sexuality. An essential component of any treatment program must be sex education. The victim of abuse must have the opportunity to ask questions and to correct distorted information about sex. The family has already proven itself to be inadequate in providing sex education to victims of sexual abuse. Individual or small group meetings with a nurse or health educator are the first steps toward reeducating the confused victim.

COUNSELING SERVICES

Counseling is a service that is frequently misunderstood. If you go to your school counselor to have your schedule changed, you are not receiving counseling. If your counselor suggests that you enroll in Spanish, rather than French, you are not receiving counseling. If your counselor lectures you about being late, cutting classes, or talking back to teachers, you are not receiving counseling. Although all of these things might happen in a counselor's office, they are guidance activities rather than counseling.

In a counseling relationship, you as the client decide what you want to share with your counselor. What you want to say, what you want to change, and how you choose to change are all determined by you. The counselor is there to listen to you rather than to tell you what to do. Underlying the counselor-client relationship is the counselor's strong belief that you have the ability to reach your own decisions. The counselor is there to listen, to question, to encourage you as you struggle, and to support you as you make the choices with which you are comfortable.

The counselor with whom you work will probably not be

your school counselor. It is likely that you will be assigned
to a counselor who works in a mental health agency or the
protective service agency to which abuse reports are made.
Some juvenile courts have their own court-appointed
counselors who work primarily with victims of sexual
abuse. The counseling program includes a variety of counseling opportunities.

Individual Counseling

Some victims of sexual abuse may have spoken with
counselors before but may not have been involved in a
counseling relationship. Other victims may have never
spoken with any kind of counselor prior to the abuse. They
may be afraid that they will not say or do what is expected
of them.

One of the major aspects of the counselor-client relationship is trust. If you have been a victim of sexual abuse, the
father you trusted to take care of you and the mother you
expected to protect you have both let you down. It is
understandable that you may be extremely hesitant to trust
any adult. Counselors who work with sexual abuse survivors know that it may take weeks before the survivor is
able to talk about what has happened. Coupled with this
lack of trust may be fear of rejection or disapproval by the
counselor. As a victim you may be thinking, "If I tell the
counselor what I did, s/he won't like me. I'm a bad person." Nothing could be farther from the truth. The counselor is not there to judge you. By being open and honest
with your counselor, you can help yourself get past the
painful experiences. The trained counselor is aware that
the total responsibility for the sexual abuse rests with the
adults in your life.

In individual counseling you have the opportunity to express your feelings about the abuse and its effects on you and other family members. For those who have difficulty talking directly about sexual abuse, skilled counselors use special techniques to make it easier for them to express their feelings. One such technique is the use of play materials. Children, in particular, may describe what happened using puppets, anatomically correct dolls, or dollhouse figures. Art materials such as clay, finger paints, markers, or crayons may be used to speak for the victim of any age. Some victims are more at ease writing their story or writing poems or journals about the molestation and its effects.

There are also books about sexual abuse that the counselor may read with or to the victim. A discussion of the story in the book may help the victim to share a personal story. As the client becomes more accustomed to the counseling experience, decisions about changes in life-style become easier. Just as each abusive situation is different, so is the time needed for individual counseling. Short-term counseling may be adequate for the person who was molested once sometime ago by a distant relative. The more common situation is one in which the daughter was molested for five or more years by her father or a father substitute. That victim is likely to require a longer program of individual counseling.

Group Counseling

No matter how many articles and books are written about sexual abuse, victims are inclined to feel that no one else has been victimized in the same way. In groups composed of victims in the same age category, each member realizes that indeed others have experienced similar abuse and can understand the pain and turmoil associated with it. Group members learn from one another and from the counselor who leads the group. They learn how to express their emotions in a positive way, how to stand up for themselves, how to cope with potential abusers, and how to deal effectively with other family members. In many instances, group members have felt that they were different and did not fit in with others their age. This sense of alienation from peers has resulted in limited social contacts. The group provides a safe environment in which to practice socialization skills. As members learn to relate to one another, they learn to relate to peers outside of the group.

For many members the group may also be a place to practice for an eventual confrontation with their abuser. Difficult as confrontation may be, it is necessary if the family is ever to be totally reunited. Through role-playing and role rehearsal, members can prepare for this meeting. Group members can provide instant feedback and suggest alternatives to each other. They also supply support and encouragement to other members as they encounter new challenges or obstacles related to the abuse.

Group counseling can occur while the victims are also involved in individual counseling. Usually it takes many individual sessions before a client is ready for a group. The individual counseling may continue during the period of group counseling and after group counseling ends. In many settings the leader of the group is not the same person with whom the client works in individual counseling.

Group counseling is not for everyone. An extremely shy or highly emotional client may be uncomfortable in a counseling group. A client who cannot listen to others or who is unwilling to attempt to help others is likely to be dissatisfied with group counseling. For the majority of sexual abuse victims, however, a group counseling experience can be extremely helpful in preparing them to relate to others in a more positive manner.

Mother/daughter or Mother/son Counseling

Although our focus is on services for victims of sexual abuse, it should be pointed out that an effective treatment program includes counseling for both parents as well. At the same time that the victim is in counseling, mothers and fathers should also be in counseling.

As indicated earlier, the father is the most common abuser in a sexually abusive family. His victim is most likely to be his daughter but may be his son. In either situation the victims often bear great resentment toward the mother for not protecting them from the abuse. In many families the relationship between mother and victim has been poor for a long time. Indicative of this negative relationship are such victim comments as, "We've never been close," or, "I've never been able to talk to my mother," or, "I've never been able to please her. She always favors my sister."

If the victim is to remain in the home with the mother, much work must be done on the mother/daughter or mother/son relationship. In some situations the hostility between mother and child is so great that the victim must remain in foster care rather than risk returning home. Even under these circumstances, an attempt should be made to provide counseling for the mother and child together. A major expectation of this counseling is that the mother will admit her failure to protect her child. If instead she blames the victim or refuses to believe the victim, reuniting the family may be impossible.

Father/daughter or Father/son Counseling

Not all victims are willing or able to participate in ongoing counseling sessions with their abuser. Even one such meeting requires an extensive foundation of individual counseling for victim and perpetrator. The goal of this meeting would be to have the perpetrator accept total responsibility for the abuse. The victim has heard from others that the abuse was not her fault. She is most likely to believe this when she hears it from her abuser.

If the victim chooses to continue counseling sessions with the abuser, the sessions focus on redefining the victim-abuser relationship. These sessions should never be forced on the victim. The victim should have the right to decide whether or not to confront the abuser. This is the complete opposite of the way the power was distributed in the abuse situation. The experience of finally being in control is an important part of the victim's healing process.

The stories of two abuse victims who arrived at different decisions about confronting their abuser may clarify the way such decisions are reached.

Anne's father had been her best friend in her family. Long before the abuse started, Anne and her dad had a special bond: They shared an interest in science. Every science project or school science fair provided an opportunity for them to work and study together. No one else in the family seemed interested in these activities, but her dad was always there to help and cheer Anne on. After the abuse was reported, the father was sentenced to a six-month work-release program. He was not allowed to contact Anne. Although Anne was very relieved that the abuse had ended, she missed her father. She was in an honors chemistry class at high school and was excited about the many challenges it presented.

Anne told her counselor how much she missed sharing her scientific interest with her father, and the counselor asked if Anne would like to talk with him. Anne had mixed feelings about seeing her father. She was still angry with him about the abuse, but she missed the positive parts of their relationship. After thinking it over, Anne decided that she would like to see her father, knowing that her counselor would be with her for the meeting.

When they gathered in the counselor's office, things were very awkward for the first few moments. Anne did not know what to say. Her father couldn't seem to speak above a whisper. Finally he told his daughter how bad he felt that he had abused her. He said it was all his fault and that he wanted to learn how to be the best father for her. Anne cried. He cried. They agreed that they wanted to work on their relationship. Both left the meeting feeling that they could make a new start toward a real father-daughter relationship.

Unlike Anne, Louise decided that she did not want to meet with her abuser. Her mother had divorced her stepfather after the abuse was reported. Her stepfather had often threatened to harm Louise and her sisters if they resisted his abuse. He had moved to another state after the divorce. Louise felt much safer knowing that he was far away. She had some things she wanted to say to her stepfather and some questions that she wanted to ask him, but she was not willing to see him. Her counselor helped her express her feelings in a variety of ways. Louise was encouraged to write a letter to her stepfather, saying everything that she wanted to say. Instead of mailing the letter, she brought it to read to her counseling group. Saying out loud what she wanted to say and punching a pillow until she was physically exhausted helped Louise get rid of her anger in the safety of her group. Like Anne, she experienced a great sense of relief.

Triad Counseling

Triad counseling means counseling with the mother, father, and victim together. If the family is to function as a family again, this is a crucial step in reorganizing roles and responsibilities. In triad counseling each family member participates in defining the roles of the other members. The victim, who has frequently been used as an adult substitute, has the opportunity to become a child again. The adults, who have abdicated their parental roles, reclaim them.

Family Counseling

In family counseling all members of the immediate family gather together to work on problems that are part of the family. Sexual abuse and the aftermath of reporting have resulted in changes for all members. Problems related to how each sibling reacts to the victim and to each parent can be resolved in family counseling. If, as a result of triad counseling, some family members have agreed to take on new roles, family counseling provides an opportunity to explain and further define those roles.

SUMMARY

The many varieties of counseling available to victims of sexual abuse can provide the support system necessary to deal with the abuse and to put it in the past. Individual and group counseling have proven to be especially helpful to victims. Counseling with other family members can bring about improved family communication.

DISCUSSION TOPICS

1. Do you think that counseling is really necessary for victims of sexual abuse? Why or why not?
2. What counseling resources are available for victims in your community?
3. If you were a victim of sexual abuse, what do you think you would want to say to your abuser?
4. How does sexual abuse affect other family members?
5. What would be some of your concerns about sharing information in group counseling?
6. Should a perpetrator be forced to meet with his victim if he does not want to?
7. Obtain a copy of the United Nations Declaration of the Rights of the Child. How does this document relate to victims of sexual abuse?

CHAPTER VIII

Questions About Reporting

Every state in the United States has a law requiring certain people who come in contact with children and adolescents to report suspected cases of sexual abuse to the state child protection agency. Physicians, teachers, school counselors, school social workers, and nurses are some of the people usually required by law to report.

If you are a victim of sexual abuse and still in danger of being abused, it is essential that you share this information with someone who will report it. You can also report the abuse yourself by calling the number listed in the front of your phonebook under "Child Abuse." You may be a friend of someone who is being abused. Encourage that person to share the secret with someone who will report it. Reporting is the first step to getting help for a troubled family.

In this chapter we consider how to report abuse, the aftermath of reporting, and self-protection issues.

How do I report sexual abuse?

There are several ways to report sexual abuse. If you have access to a school counselor or school social worker, make an appointment to talk with this person and let him or her know what is happening to you. If you have a favorite teacher with whom you would be more comfortable, you might take the teacher to your meeting with the counselor, or you could seek out a private time to share your story with the teacher.

Sometimes adolescents are inclined to share things with friends rather than adults. If that has happened to you, encourage your friend to talk with someone who will report the abuse. You might offer to go along when your friend talks to the counselor or social worker.

Another resource that is available to you is the police department. Police officers are also mandated reporters. They must notify the state protective services agency about cases of abuse. Unlike schools, police departments do not close down for vacation periods. Thus someone is available to take reports twenty-four hours a day.

You may also choose to tell your mother or some other adult relative about the abuse. Be prepared for the possibility that family members may not believe you. They are accustomed to thinking of your abuser in a certain way. Seeing him in a different light may be initially too difficult for those who love him to accept. They may attempt to defend the abuser or try to convince you that you are imagining things. They may even suggest that you forget about the abuse and not mention it to anyone. Not telling will probably mean that the abuse will go on.

CONTINUE TELLING PEOPLE IN AUTHORITY ABOUT THE ABUSE UNTIL SOMEONE BELIEVES YOU AND REPORTS IT!

Why is it necessary to report?

Sexual abuse occurs in families where there are many problems. Those problems, like the abuse, have probably been present for a long time. Much as children would like to be able to "fix" their family's problems, they cannot do that. For families to get the help they need, it is necessary to notify someone about the abuse.

If you are being victimized in your family and are close to high school graduation, you may be thinking that you will soon escape the abuse by moving away or living at college. If you will soon be leaving, you may be reluctant to report. However, keep in mind that while the abuse may soon be ending for you, the same is not true for any sisters or brothers who are still at home. You may be safely away, but your brothers and sisters at home are going to be abused.

Perhaps you are the last minor living at home. Think of reporting as a way of protecting your younger nieces, nephews, and cousins from sexual abuse. Unless someone stops your abuser, he or she will continue to be a threat to you and to other family members.

What happens after I report?

The answer to that question differs somewhat from state to state. In general it can be stated that there will be an investigation of your charges. A protective service worker or a police officer or both will interview you to find out the specific charges that you are making. The investigator will usually try to talk with you at school or somewhere else away from your home. This protects you from being interrupted or bothered by family members.

One of several things may happen next. Your abuser may be arrested, charged, and required to post bond. He may be ordered to move out of the house immediately. If he cannot post bond he may be kept in jail until his case goes to court. The protective services worker may accompany you to your house to tell your mother about the abuse. If your mother does not believe you or shows hostility toward you, the protective services worker may decide that it is not safe for you to be at home. You may be temporarily placed in foster care or a group home. In some states you would be temporarily placed in foster care regardless of your mother's reaction, to give the protective service workers time to evaluate your home environment. In either case the goal would be to return you to your home as soon as possible.

Will my dad lose his job?

Not necessarily. If he can post bond he will not be in jail. Therefore he can continue working and supporting his family. There is no guarantee, however, that someone at work won't find out what has happened. In small communities it is especially difficult to keep such charges a secret.

If he is convicted of the charges of sexual abuse, your father may spend time in prison. Some states provide work-release programs for abusers, allowing participants to work during the day and return to prison at night.

If the abuser loses his job because of the charges against him, it is crucial to realize that the responsibility for that loss rests solely with him. You did not cause the abuse; you did not will it to continue. He made the choice to risk his job, his family, his place in the community, and his child's love and respect. He made the wrong choice and must accept the consequences of that choice.

How will others in my family treat me?

That is a very difficult question. Probably the best indication of how they will treat you is your past experience with them. If you were not close to your brothers and sisters, it is unlikely that this experience will make you closer. If you and your mother barely spoke to each other, it is likely that communication will be even more strained. However, counseling sessions for you and for other family members can result in an improved relationship between you and your family.

Do I have to go for counseling?

Consider the effects of sexual abuse listed in the preceding chapter. You probably are experiencing some of those effects, even though the abuse has ended. It is possible that other emotional issues will come up in later years. It is also possible that, with a strong support system of family and friends, you might be able to deal with the many ramifications of abuse. The question then might be better stated as, "Why should you have to struggle with these issues without professional help?"

Let us assume that your goal is to eliminate any hangups resulting from sexual abuse. In individual or group counseling you will receive feedback on what problems are present and how close you are coming to your goal. You will have someone who will consistently support you in your attempts to learn new behavior. Counselors will not tell you what to do; they will help you to figure out what you want to do.

Compare choosing counseling to help you achieve your goal with choosing a means to get from Chicago to Milwaukee. Your goal is to get to Milwaukee. You have several ways of getting there. If you had no other choice, you could even walk. Walking would enable you to achieve your goal. However, it would take longer than flying or driving; it would result in more personal discomfort; and it would present more danger. The possibility of setbacks would be greater. There would be a higher risk of getting lost. All of these factors are inherent in not getting counseling. Without counseling you might still reach your goal, but it would be a longer, more difficult, and more dangerous journey.

How can I find a counselor who understands sexual abuse?

The human services agency to whom the abuse was reported should have a list of counselors who are experienced in counseling survivors of sexual abuse. Some areas have Daughters and Sons United groups for children who have been abused. As mentioned earlier, there are various sponsors for groups of adults who were molested as children.

How long will it take for my family to get back to normal?

That is impossible to say. Things may never be the same in your family, but they may be better than they were when the abuse was going on. The problems in your family have been there for a long time and will take time to be remedied. How willing your family members are to work on the problem will determine how long it will take to rebuild your family.

My dad keeps promising that the abuse will stop. Why doesn't it?

It is doubtful that abuse will stop on its own. When your father makes these promises, he may really mean them. However, like an alcoholic or a smoker, he has developed a habit that is very difficult to break. If he stops molesting you, it is probable that he is molesting someone else in your family. Reporting him is the first step in stopping the abuse.

I'd like to tell my school counselor about this, but I don't want her to report it. Can I do that?

Before I answer that, I would like you to think about why you would tell your counselor. I suspect it is because you want her to help you do something that you cannot do by yourself. That is, you want her to help you stop the abuse. The only way that she can do that is to report it to the state child protective services. She cannot come to your house or call your father and tell him to stop. She has only one choice. The answer to your question is *No*. Every state has a law requiring school personnel, including counselors, to report suspected cases of abuse and neglect. She would be breaking that law if she did not report the abuse. States have a variety of penalties for failure to report. If your counselor did not make a report, she could lose her job or be fined or even serve time in a county jail.

Once the report is made, your counselor can continue to be a resource for you as you work through the reporting process. Telling your counselor is the first step toward getting help for your family.

I told Mom what Dad has been doing. She slapped me across the face and told me never to say anything like that again. Why won't she help me?

That is a difficult question to answer. Many adult women whom I have known recount a similar experience.

While I cannot comment on your specific circumstances, there seem to be several reasons why mothers, when told about abuse, fail to act. Sometimes it is fear of the spouse. The husband may be physically abusive to the wife, making her afraid to challenge anything he does or says. Or the mother may be economically dependent and afraid that speaking out would mean loss of her home and your father's financial support. Still other mothers were sexually abused as children. They could not stop the abuse then, and they feel powerless to stop it now. Some accept it as the way families are. It is also possible that the whole idea is so upsetting to her that she wants to ignore it in the hope that it will disappear.

There may be other reasons why she did not react the way you had hoped. I suggest that you approach the subject with your mother again. Find a time when no one else is around and you can get her full attention. Lead into it gradually, rather than blurting it out. One way to start might be, "Mom, there's something very important that I need to talk to you about. It's been bothering me for a long time and I need your help with it. I know this is going to be hard for you to hear. It's very hard for me to tell you. For a long time Dad has been..."

I cannot promise that your mother will help you. If she does not, then you must tell someone in authority what is happening. Keep telling until you are believed and the report is made.

I cannot bring myself to report the sexual abuse that I am experiencing. What else can I do to stop being a victim?

I would again encourage you to bring the abuse to the attention of someone who will report it. That is the most successful way to stop it. However, I realize that some victims find it impossible to report. You should be aware that there are some risks in trying to stop the abuse on your own. You may not be able to stop it no matter what you try. By making an attempt, you may antagonize your abuser and he may become physically abusive to you. If you try to avoid him, he may find many ways of punishing you. With these warnings in mind, I would suggest that you do the following:

1. *Try to figure out if there is any schedule or pattern to the abuse.* For instance, does it happen only at night or only on certain nights? Where does it happen? Who else is home when it happens? If there is a pattern, it is easier to plan a defensive strategy. If there is no pattern, defensive alternatives must be ready at all times.
2. *Identify ways to avoid your abuser.* Think about safe places where you could go to avoid being alone with your abuser. Also, consider which friends could spend time at your house and when they could be there.
3. *Develop outside interests that keep you away from home at high-risk times.* Be aware that if you avoid high-risk times, your abuser will attempt to revise his pattern. Therefore you cannot relax your vigilance when the abuser is nearby.
4. *Reconsider reporting.* What is the major obstacle to reporting? What do you fear will occur when the report is made? Is that worse than continuing to be sexually abused?

Let us consider Patti's approach to stopping her father from molesting her. She has realized that her father approaches her only when her mother is at work. Saturdays and Monday nights are high-risk times for abuse. Although Patti is not old enough for a real job, she was able to arrange a mother's helper job on Saturdays. She has started going directly to the library after school on Mondays; her mother picks her up at 9:00 p.m. on her way home from work. If she thinks that her father is at home alone at other times, she brings a friend home to study with her. Her father has been very sarcastic toward her since she began this self-protection campaign. He is talking about cutting her allowance since she's not around to clean house as much as she had been in the past. She fears that he will still find a way to molest her.

While Patti may have halted the abuse temporarily, it is unlikely that her father will give up. In the meantime Patti is afraid of being in her own home and resentful of the time she must spend away from home. Until the abuse is reported, the fear will continue.

My best friend's father and brother have been sexually abusing her. She's really afraid of them. When she told me about it, she made me promise not to tell anyone. I don't want to break a promise, but I'm really worried about her. She's talking about running away. What can I do?

First of all, you must understand that your friend is in a situation that will not improve on its own. Running away poses many dangers and is no solution. Obviously she trusts you and needs your support. Tell her that you made a promise that you can't keep. Encourage her to talk to the school counselor or nurse. Let her know that you will go with her if she wishes. If she refuses, you have no choice. Report the abuse to the school counselor or nurse. Be prepared for the possibility that your friend may be angry with you. You risk losing a friend as you help her, but if she runs away you might lose her permanently.

SUMMARY

Reporting is the first step toward getting help for an abusive family. Abuse is an adult problem. It is unlikely that children or adolescents can stop the abuse without adult assistance. Those who attempt to stop the abuse alone may risk additional abuse. Reporting the abuse to a counselor or other mandated reporter is the most certain way of stopping it.

DISCUSSION TOPICS

1. What are some other ways that Patti might use to avoid the abuse?

CHAPTER IX

The Adolescent Abuser

Much of our attention thus far has been directed to father-daughter sexual abuse. As awareness of sexual abuse has increased, so has the realization that sexual abusers are not always adults. This chapter considers the adolescent who molests children. The masculine pronoun is used because the vast majority of adolescent abusers are male. However, as in all other categories of abuse, there are female adolescents who molest children.

THE CYCLE

Many adult sexual abusers and pedophiles have histories of sexual victimization as children or adolescents. It is difficult for most of us to understand how someone who knows the pain of being a victim can become a perpetrator. Logic suggests that a victim would be the least likely to become a perpetrator.

Unfortunately, logic and abuse have nothing in common. On the contrary, the pattern of victim turning into victimizer is widely prevalent. Perhaps the story of Kyle will clarify the process.

Kyle was fifteen when he was arrested for molesting a nine-year-old neighbor boy. To the inevitable question "Why?" Kyle's response was that he wanted to know what it was like to be in charge for a change. Upon further questioning, Kyle described the abuse he had experienced over a four-year period by his high school shop teacher. Kyle lacked any apparent concern for his victim. "It was no big deal," he said,—certainly nothing like what he had endured.

The story of Kyle is typical in many ways. Like many more male than female victims, he was molested by someone outside of his family. His abuser was of the same sex, making it very unlikely that he would have told anyone about it. He identified with his abuser and wanted to have the same sense of power and control over someone that his abuser had over him. When caught he was more surprised than remorseful.

Sometimes adults are inclined to dismiss behavior like Kyle's as harmless sexual experimentation. Underestimating its seriousness has resulted in a continuation of abusive incidents by untreated adolescent offenders. Too often families attempt to resolve the problem without professional intervention. The abuser's family agrees to "keep my kid away from your kid," and that is the end of discussion in either household. In most instances, however, that is not the end of the abuse. The abuser will probably find other victims, perhaps a younger sibling.

OTHER PATTERNS

Scott was twelve when he began baby-sitting for two little girls who lived across the street. One of the benefits of the job was that the family had cable television, which his parents refused to have installed. After his young charges were asleep, Scott watched the kinds of movies that were forbidden in his home. "Trying out" some of the sexual techniques he saw, he molested both little girls, telling

them that it was a secret game. Scott's baby-sitting career
came to an abrupt end when the girls' preschool teacher
told their mother about the baby-sitter's game.

Scott's situation was very different from Kyle's. Scott had
never been molested. His sexual feelings were new and
surprising to him. The baby-sitting job provided him with
access to young children. Cable television provided him with
instruction. In this scenario Scott could as well have been
Sally or Susie. Sexual abuse by young baby-sitters is not
uncommon.

Adolescence is a time when peer pressure is extremely
strong. Teens want to belong to a group and be accepted.
Bill and Greg had been fondling their five-year-old sister for
some time. They played sex games with her and invited their
friend Steve to participate. Steve was hesitant but did not
want his friends to think he was chicken. He rationalized
that a five-year-old wouldn't know what was going on and
wouldn't remember it later.

In some cases adolescents have been violent toward young
sexual abuse victims; in a few instances children have been
killed.

Sibling Abuse

Although statistics do not confirm the theory, many
professionals suspect that sibling abuse is the most common
form of sexual abuse. The pattern may be one of same-sex
abuse, heterosexual abuse, or a combination. Consider the
story of Marcia, who was molested by her three older
brothers. The abuse began when Marcia was in first grade
and continued until each brother came of age and moved
out of the house. Marcia's father had abandoned the family
soon after she was born. Her brothers provided the only

money that supplemented the family's welfare check.
Marcia's mother called the boys the men of the house. She
refused to listen to her daughter's complaints. Years later
Marcia learned that her oldest brother had also molested
the other two boys.

Sibling abusers sometimes claim that they are teaching
their victims rather than molesting them. Chuck's older
sister was very popular in their high school. As a freshman
he had to cope with teachers' comparisons of his
accomplishments with those of Alice, a junior. In some
ways Chuck was jealous of Alice, but he was also proud of
her. Chuck was the opposite of Alice in many ways. She
was outgoing, he was shy. She was attractive, he was
dealing unsuccessfully with teenage acne. She had many
friends; he had few. Alice taught Chuck how to dance, how
to decline Latin nouns, and how to write a term paper.
Finally she decided that it was her responsibility to teach
him about sex. When Chuck protested she reminded him
that he needed her help in making it in high school.

Both Marcia and Chuck were betrayed by their older
siblings. Neither could enlist the support or understanding
of their parents. Marcia's mother would not listen to her
complaints. Chuck's parents owned a business that kept
them away from home, and they left Alice in charge. The
abusive siblings were in an almost parental role: They were
to be obeyed without question.

Satanic Cults and Adolescent Sexual Abuse

In the past several years the incidence of sexual abuse
cases with satanic involvement has risen. Many day-care
cases have involved testimony about abusers in robes and
masks and other cult trappings. Young children have

described rituals, chanting, animal sacrifices, and satanic symbols in conjunction with their molestation. Multiple victims and multiple perpetrators have been involved. More female than male abusers have been prosecuted in such cases.

The similarity of descriptions of ritualistic abuse in many areas of the United States seems to verify the existence of satanic-sponsored sexual abuse of children. What cannot be verified, however, is whether the perpetrators are members of satanic groups or simply skilled in techniques to frighten children into silence.

Devil worship has been a reality since before the birth of Christ. Alienated, isolated teenagers are prime candidates for satanic cults. They are also prime candidates for sexual abuse by the members. Typically a teenager is invited to a party where alcohol, drugs, and sex are on the agenda. The "guest" is photographed or videotaped in compromising situations. Later he or she is coerced to join the group under threat of having the pictures revealed to parents or peers.

Does joining such a group mean that the adolescent will become a sexual abuser? Not necessarily. There are several possibilities. The adolescent may already have been sexually abusive, and joining the cult serves to endorse or affirm that behavior. The satanic group did not turn him into a molester; it accepted him as a molester. The other scenario is that joining such a group relieves a potential abuser of barriers to abuse such as a sense of guilt or concern for the child victim. The new member senses permission or even a directive to do whatever he wants to anyone, including children.

No accurate statistics are available on adolescents involved in cults. Certainly not all of them are involved in child sexual abuse. However, the cult environment is accepting and, in some cases, encouraging of such offenses.

CHARACTERISTICS OF THE ADOLESCENT ABUSER

Although each case of sexual abuse by an adolescent is unique, certain characteristics are shared by many offenders. These include:

1. *Low self-esteem.*
The abusive adolescent may experience little success academically or in peer relationships. He or she may feel not as good or not as attractive as others.

2. *Social isolation.*
The adolescent does not feel a part of any group in school. He or she does not fit in with the "brains" or the "jocks" or other established groups. Social skills may be limited. Adults may have the impression that he or she has friends because of membership in an organization or on a team. Closer scrutiny reveals, however, that membership does not equal friendship.

3. *Lack of information about sexuality.*
Abusive adolescents may come from a restrictive home in which sex is never discussed and questions are never answered. Conversely, they may come from a chaotic environment in which sexual boundaries are relaxed or nonexistent.

4. *History of abuse or neglect.*
Many abusive adolescents have experienced physical or sexual abuse or neglect in their own family. They may

believe that all families function like their own and that abuse or neglect are part of everyone's life.

5. *Lack of parental support and attention.*

In sibling abuse, the abusive adolescent is often in the role of substitute parent. Parents who are overwhelmed with their own problems may not realize that they are expecting too much of the teen placed in the caretaker role.

The adolescent who abuses children outside the family may lack adequate communication with the parents.

6. *Difficulty expressing anger.*

Adolescent offenders are filled with anger and hostility that they express inappropriately.

7. *Other problems.*

The adolescent abuser may have academic deficiencies, physical problems, substance abuse problems, or many other personal difficulties.

TREATMENT

The public has been slow in recognizing the actuality of the adolescent sexual abuser. Thus, fewer treatment programs are available for them than for adult abusers. Treatment settings include:

1. *Offices of private practitioners.*

Especially if the adolescent abuser does not have a history of abusive behavior, the services of a counselor, social worker, or psychologist in private practice may be an option. Courts are inclined to recommend counseling rather than incarceration if the abusive adolescent has no record of aggressive behavior and has a supportive family environment.

2. *Community-based outpatient program.*

These programs offer individual and group counseling, family counseling, and, in some cases, support groups for victims of adolescent abuse. The program may also have an educational segment for those who need academic tutoring or job training.

3. *Hospital setting.*

The adolescent abuser who is addicted to drugs or alcohol must first control those addictions before the sexual abuse can be considered. The offender who is suffering from mental illness may also benefit from treatment in a medical facility. Treatment consists of intensive individual, group, and family counseling. Because the patient is in residence, medication and behavior can be monitored. The adolescent who does not have a positive family environment can make progress while separated from family members.

4. *Residential treatment programs.*

In residential programs adolescent abusers live away from home for several weeks, months, or even years. Residential centers are either self-contained or linked with other community resources. In the latter case, the offender receives counseling and educational services outside the facility.

5. *Correctional facilities.*

If an adolescent abuser has been prosecuted for sexual abuse, he or she may be sentenced to a correctional facility. Few treatment programs for young offenders exist in such facilities.

The treatment of adolescent abusers is a comparatively new phenomenon. The objective is to prevent child molestation from becoming a lifelong pattern. It is too early to know how successful treatment programs and techniques are in meeting that objective.

LET'S SUPPOSE

Let's suppose that you are an adolescent who has been thinking about touching a younger child sexually. What should you do? That depends on how frequently such thoughts occur. If sexual contact with a child has come to mind briefly once or twice and your reaction has been "No way!", you have nothing to worry about.

If, however, such thoughts occupy more and more of your time or if they just won't go away, there is a possible problem. As you have no doubt noticed, throughout this book I have recommended that you talk with your school counselor. In this instance I do not make that recommendation, at least not at first. I suggest instead that you broach the subject with your parents. That may be difficult for you to do. However, you need their assistance in getting professional help before you act on your impulses. Many communities have trained sex therapists who can help you. Your parents may ask a hospital for a referral to someone who specializes in working with adolescents. Your family physician is another resource who can refer you to a therapist.

If your parents cannot help you to obtain counseling, you must rely on the school counselor or social worker. It is imperative that you share these thoughts with a professional who can assist you. Without help the danger is that you will eventually act on them.

Let's suppose that you have crossed the line between thought and action. If you have engaged in sexual activity with a child, you must seek professional help immediately.

Your community may have a hotline that you can call for
information about local resources. You can also call the
reporting number listed for your state in the Appendix.
Youth service agencies are another source of information
about treatment programs and professionals in your area.

SUMMARY

Adolescence is often a confusing and tumultuous time.
The added burden of being sexually involved with children
can be overwhelming. There are programs and support
services for those who have the courage to seek help.
Without treatment the adolescent abuser runs a high risk of
becoming an adult abuser. The cycle can be broken, and
treatment provides the opportunity to rewrite expectations.

DISCUSSION TOPICS

1. Identify the treatment resources for adolescent
   abusers in your community.
2. What would you do if you found out that your friend
   was molesting her or his brother?
3. Do you think that boys should baby-sit outside the
   family? Why or why not?
4. Discuss cults and cult activity in your community. Is
   there evidence that cults exist?
5. Can adolescents who molest children go on to live
   normal adult lives?
6. What were Steve's alternatives when pressured by his
   friends?
7. What can schools do to prevent adolescents from
   becoming abusers? What can families do?

CHAPTER X

Prevention: The Adolescent's Role

In recent history we have witnessed the conquest of many childhood diseases. Great strides have been made against various forms of cancer including leukemia. Vaccines prevent measles, diphtheria, influenza, and polio. We are encouraged by reports that researchers are moving closer to cures for cystic fibrosis and muscular dystrophy.

But sexual abuse in not a disease. No vaccine nor medical breakthrough will result in a cure. That is both bad and good news. It is bad news in that we would all applaud a quick and dramatic solution to sexual abuse. It is good news in that we are not facing medical obstacles that could require years of research.

Sexual abuse of children is a learned behavior. As such it can be controlled and changed. Society has been reluctant to acknowledge the reality of sexual abuse and thus has done little to prevent it. This chapter considers some of the steps that could lead to the elimination of sexual abuse.

RESPONSIBILITY

The responsibility for sexual abuse lies first with the perpetrator. Despite the rationalizations made by offenders when discovered, the victim is never responsible. Sexual abusers act as a result of a conscious decision. The decision may be based upon a variety of circumstances, illogical thoughts, or feelings. The fact remains, however, that the abuser decides to molest or not molest.

Responsibility also rests with adults who have reason to believe that someone is a danger to children but do nothing about it. All of the following are examples in which an adult failed to protect a child or children.

Ken L. molested his daughter from the time she was a toddler until she was in junior high and told the school counselor what was happening. Over the years there had been many indications that the father-daughter relationship was unusual. Carol's mother came home early from work one day and saw her scantily dressed husband emerging from Carol's room. He explained that he had been about to take a shower when he thought he heard his daughter call out. Another time Carol's younger brother told his mother that Carol and the father had been in her room with the door locked. Carol's father took her with him whenever he went on the briefest errand. Her brother always asked to go along but was never included. When Carol was twelve her mother heard her shouting at her father to stay out of her room. At first Mrs. L. thought her husband was waking Carol to get ready for school. When she realized that it was 5:00 a.m., her husband said he had misread the clock. Mrs. L. scolded her daughter for being so rude to her father. Carol told her mother the truth. Her mother was shocked at first, then angry with Carol for saying such terrible things. She warned Carol that if she made up any more stories she would be sent to boarding school. A few weeks later Carol confided in the school counselor.

Mr. Harvey had taught at Smithfield Junior High for fifteen years. Girl students complained to their friends that he was overly friendly and made sexual comments to them. Rumors about him circulated among students and staff for years. When a new principal was assigned to Smithfield, the rumors were running rampant. Mr. Harvey had been inviting students to come to his house on weekends for "tutoring." The new principal decided that Mr. Harvey was a liability. He had him transferred to a fifth-grade opening across town, reasoning that Mr. Harvey would be less of a problem around younger children.

Stan and Kathy had two young children and many unpaid bills. They agreed that Kathy would have to get a full-time job, but child care was a major concern. It did not make sense for Kathy to work, only to have most of her income go to child care. They found what might seem an ideal solution. Kathy's father, who had recently retired, was very willing to baby-sit for his grandchildren. Kathy was less enthusiastic about the idea than her husband was. She had never told Stan that her father had molested her when she was a child. After some thought, however, she agreed to the plan, reasoning that her father would not dare do anything to her children. After all, they were his only grandchildren and his only family since his wife's death. Kathy was certain that her father would not risk losing his family.

Martin was a counselor in an adolescent treatment program. He had excellent counseling skills and was known for his ability to work with the most hostile and belligerent clients. However, several clients complained that Martin had made sexual advances to them. The counselor in the office next to Martin's expressed similar concerns about him. The director confronted Martin with the accusations of clients and his colleague. He and Martin agreed that Martin would quietly resign. The agency would thus avoid scandal and

Martin's reputation would not be tarnished. The director agreed to give Martin a favorable recommendation. Martin moved several states away and took a job in a similar agency working with adolescents.

Molly is a caseworker for her state's protective service department. Her job is to provide follow-up services for families in which children have been sexually abused. She is expected to monitor her caseload of eighty families, making certain that no further sexual abuse occurs and that the families follow the court's orders. Molly often works twelve hours a day and comes to work on weekends just to keep up with the paperwork. Funds that were earmarked for hiring more caseworkers have been diverted to finance a new highway.

In each of these situations someone in addition to the perpetrator failed to protect a child or children. Carol's mother accepted any explanation that would allow her to ignore her husband's behavior. Both the Smithfield principal and the agency director were primarily concerned with getting rid of the perpetrator quickly and quietly. Kathy was so desperate for a baby-sitter that she lied to herself about her father.

The example of Molly is somewhat different. Molly is not failing to protect children. On the contrary, she is working extremely hard to protect them. However, hers is an impossible task. When one of the families in her caseload comes to public attention for further sexual abuse, society will be to blame. A society that values roads or buses or buildings more than children cannot pretend to protect children.

This book is directed to adolescents who have no voice in

how tax revenues are distributed. You may think that there is nothing you can do about sexual abuse. I believe that you can take actions that will have an impact on the eradication of sexual abuse. Let's consider some of your options.

WHAT YOU CAN DO

Report

Reporting sexual abuse or attempted sexual abuse is a way to protect others. If you have been molested by someone in your family, it is likely that others are at risk. The same is true if you were molested by someone outside your family. The molestations will continue unless you report.

Educate Yourself about the Problem

You have already begun to do that by reading this book. Contact the protective services department in your state or province for current statistics. How many cases of sexual abuse were reported in the last year? What was the average age of the victim? Of the perpetrator? What happens to sexual abusers? Ask for a copy of the department's annual report, which should include most of this information.

Talk with Others about the Problem

An informed opinion merits respect and attention. Share your concerns about sexual abuse in your community. Perhaps you belong to a group at school or church in which social concerns are discussed. You may have the opportunity to use a class as your forum. Perhaps you will be assigned to make a speech in a communications class or to do a term project. If you are comfortable doing so, talk with your parents about what you have learned about sexual abuse.

Identify Others Who Share Your Concern

Some who hear you talk about sexual abuse may not want to think about such a thing. Some may say you are too young to be concerned about the problem. There will be others, however, who will respond to your message and want to do something. It is this group that is likely to join with you for the next step.

Develop an Action Agenda

What problems are unique to your state or province? Are there local concerns that could be addressed? Determine your goal and the actions necessary to reach it. An action plan specifies when tasks are to be completed and who is to complete each task. Steps requiring funds are identified, and funding is pursued before the action plan gets under way.

Your group might, for example, decide to raise funds for speakers to address your school or for needed materials for a community-based treatment program. Volunteers may be needed at a crisis nursery, day-care center, or teen hotline. Treatment agencies and parent groups may need volunteer baby-sitters. There are many creative ways in which teens can take an active part in the battle against sexual abuse.

PREVENTION OF SEXUAL ABUSE

Young children need to learn about sexual abuse and what to do if they feel sexually threatened by someone. The

school is the setting in which most children can best learn
how to protect themselves.

Over the past few years many "personal safety"
programs have been used in schools. Programs have used
comic books, coloring books, films, puppets, plays, and
songs to help children recognize sexual abuse and identify
protective resources in the school or community. Some
poor programs have emphasized the "stranger as the
abuser" concept and ignored the more common situation of
a family member or trusted friend. Another inappropriate
message in some programs has been that children can "just
say no" to the abusive adult. Children cannot control
adults, and some programs imply that the *child* failed or is
at fault for not stopping the adult.

Some schools have supported programs based on myths
about sexual abuse, such as the myth that thousands of
children are kidnapped by strangers and sexually abused by
them. The truth is that most missing children were abducted
by their noncustodial parent or are runaways. Yet schools
continue to sponsor and raise funds for fingerprinting and
photographing school-aged children.

Effective personal safety programs blend into an existing
program such as sex education, health education, self-
esteem training, or affective education. That is much less
alarming to children than having a one- or two-day child
safety program separate from every other part of the school
curriculum. Good programs also stress the responsibility of
the perpetrator and never imply that the victim is responsible or could have avoided the abuse.

The best programs require advance preparation of
teachers and parents. The importance of follow-up
discussions at school and at home is emphasized. Finally,
good programs encourage children to tell someone in

authority if they have been abused or threatened with abuse. Children learn whom to tell and how to use the resources available to them. Separately from the children, parents and educators are trained to look for and deal with indications of sexual abuse.

FINAL THOUGHTS

There is much that we have to learn to better protect children from sexual abuse. The attitude that children are the property of their parents must be changed. The myths and misconceptions about sexual abuse must be dispelled. Treatment programs for the victim and the offender must be made more available. Funding for investigation, treatment, and research must be increased. Children must grow up feeling safe and secure.

The list of "musts" related to sexual abuse could take up many pages. Instead of a "must," we end with a challenge. What will be your role in making the "musts" happen?

Epilogue

You have selected this book for a variety of reasons. Perhaps curiosity about the subject prompted you to read it. You may have been assigned to read it and to write a report on it. Your concern for a friend might have motivated you to make this choice. Possibly you are a victim of sexual abuse. Regardless of why you have read this book, you may have questions or reactions that you would like to share with your parents, a teacher, or a counselor. I want to encourage you to do exactly that. If the person you talk with cannot answer your questions, together you can continue the search.

We have looked closely at sexual abuse and its effects on children and adolescents. With the information and the impressions you have acquired, you can be a resource to others who may be struggling with this problem in their lives. If you are a victim, I urge you to report the abuse. If you are a friend of a victim, I hope that you will encourage him or her to seek help. If you are concerned about abuse, find a way to share what you have learned with others in your school. Victims must learn that they are not alone and that help is available to them. Abusers must learn that their behavior will not be tolerated. Sexual abuse is a problem for all of us to solve. BE PART OF THE SOLUTION!

Appendix

The following organizations and services can be of assistance to you as you seek information about sexual abuse or wish to report it.

Local Resources:

School personnel, including teachers, counselors, social workers, psychologists, nurses, and administrators
Police officers
Librarians
Members of the clergy
Medical personnel
Rape crisis center staff members
Crisis intervention centers
YWCAs
YMCAs

State Child Protective Service Agencies and Reporting Procedures:

Alabama:
Alabama Department of Pensions and Security
Bureau of Family and Children's Services
64 North Union Street
Montgomery, AL 36130-1801
Reports made to county 24-hour emergency telephone services.

Alaska:
   Department of Health and Social Services
   Division of Family and Youth Services
   Pouch H-05
   Juneau, AK 99801
      Reports made to Division of Social Services field offices.

American Samoa:
   Government of American Samoa
   Office of the Attorney General
   Pago Pago, American Samoa 96799
      Reports made to the Department of Medical Services.

Arizona:
   Department of Economic Security
   P.O. Box 6123
   Site COE 940A
   Phoenix, AZ 85005
      Reports made to Department of Economic Security local offices.

Arkansas:
   Arkansas Department of Human Services
   Division of Social Services
   P.O. Box 1437
   Little Rock, AR 72203
      Reports made to the statewide toll-free hotline (800) 482-5964.

California:
   Office for Child Abuse Prevention
   Department of Social Services
   714-744 P Street
   Sacramento, CA 95814

Reports made to County Departments of Welfare and the Central Registry of Child Abuse (916) 445-7546, maintained by the Department of Justice.

Colorado:
Department of Social Services
1675 Sherman Street
Denver, CO 80203
Reports made to County Departments of Social Services.

Connecticut:
Connecticut Department of Children and Youth Services
Child Protective Services Department
Division of Children and Youth Services
170 Sigourney Street
Hartford, CT 06105
Reports made to (800) 842-2288.

Delaware:
Delaware Department of Health and Social Services
Division of Child Protective Services
P.O. Box 309
Wilmington, DE 19899
Reports made to statewide toll-free reporting hotline (800) 292-9582.

District of Columbia:
District of Columbia Department of Human Services
Commission on Social Services
Family Services Administration
Child Protective Services Division
First and I Streets, SW
Washington, DC 20024
Reports made to (202) 727-0995.

Florida:
  Florida Child Abuse Registry
  Central Admissions and Interstate
  1317 Winewood Boulevard
  Tallahassee, FL 32301
    Reports made to (800) 342-9152 or (904) 487-2625.

Georgia:
  Georgia Department of Human Resources
  Division of Family and Children Services
  878 Peachtree Street, NE
  Atlanta, GA 30309
    Reports made to County Departments of Family and
  Children Services.

Guam:
  Department of Public Health and Social Services
  Child Welfare Services
  Child Protective Services
  P.O. Box 2816
  Agana, Guam 96910
    Reports made to the State Child Protective Services
  Agency at 646-8417.

Hawaii:
  Department of Social Services and Housing
  Public Welfare Division
  Family and Children's Services
  P.O. Box 339
  Honolulu, HI 96809
    Reports made to the hotline operated by Kapiolani-
  Children's Medical Center on Oahu, and to branch
  offices of the Division of Hawaii, Maui, Kauai, Mokalai.

Idaho:
  Department of Health and Welfare
  Child Protection Division of Welfare
  Statehouse
  Boise, ID 83702
    Reports made to Department of Health and Welfare
  Regional Offices.

Illinois:
  Illinois Department of Children and Family Services,
    Station 509
  State Administrative Offices
  One North Old State Capitol Plaza
  Springfield, IL 62706
    Reports made to (800) 25-ABUSE.

Indiana:
  Indiana Department of Public Welfare–Child Abuse and
    Neglect
  Division of Child Welfare - Social Services
  141 South Meridian Street
  Indianapolis, IN 46225
    Reports made to County Departments of Public
  Welfare.

Iowa:
  Iowa Department of Social Services
  Division of Community Programs
  Hoover State Office Building
  Des Moines, IA 50319
    Reports made to the legally mandated toll-free report-
  ing hotline (800) 362-2178.

Kansas:
Kansas Department of Social and Rehabilitation Services
Division of Social Services
Child Protection and Family Services Section
Smith-Wilson Building
2700 West Sixth Street
Topeka, KS 66606
Reports made to Department of Social and Rehabilitation Services Area Offices.

Kentucky:
Kentucky Department of Human Resources
275 East Main Street
Frankfort, KY 40621
Reports made to County Offices within 4 regions of the State.

Louisiana:
Louisiana Department of Health and Human Resources
Office of Human Development
Baton Rouge, LA 70804
Reports made to the parish protective service units.

Maine:
Maine Department of Human Services Protective Services
Human Services Building
Augusta, ME 04333
Reports made to Regional Office or to State Agency at (800) 452-1999.

Maryland:
  Maryland Department of Human Resources
  Social Services Administration
  300 West Preston Street
  Baltimore, MD 21201
    Reports made to County Departments of Social
  Services or to local law enforcement agencies.

Massachusetts:
  Massachusetts Department of Social Services
  Protective Services
  150 Causeway Street
  Boston, MA 02114
    Reports made to Regional Offices.

Michigan:
  Michigan Department of Social Services
  Office of Children and Youth Services
  Protective Services Division
  300 South Capitol Avenue
  Lansing, MI 48926
    Reports made to County Departments of Social
  Welfare.

Minnesota:
  Minnesota Department of Public Welfare
  Department of Social Services
  Centennial Office Building
  St. Paul, MN 55155
    Reports made to the County Departments of Public
  Welfare.

Mississippi:
   Mississippi Department of Public Welfare
   Division of Social Services
   P.O. Box 352
   Jackson, MS 39216
   Reports made to (800) 222-8000.

Missouri:
   Missouri Child Abuse and Neglect Hotline
   Missouri Department of Social Services
   Division of Family Services
   DFS, P.O. Box 88
   Jefferson City, MO 65103
   Reports made to (800) 392-3738.

Montana:
   Department of Social and Rehabilitative Services
   Social Services Bureau
   P.O. Box 4210
   Helena, MT 59601
   Reports made to County Departments.

Nebraska:
   Nebraska Department of Social Services
   301 Centennial Mall South
   Lincoln, NE 68509
   Reports made to local law enforcement agencies or to
   County Divisions of Public Welfare.

Nevada:
   Department of Human Resources
   Division of Welfare
   251 Jeanell Drive, Capitol Complex
   Carson City, NV 89710
   Reports made to Division of Welfare local offices.

New Hampshire:
  New Hampshire Department of Health and Welfare
  Division of Welfare
  Bureau of Child and Family Services
  Hazen Drive
  Concord, NH 03301
    Reports made to Division of Welfare District Offices.

New Jersey:
  New Jersey Division of Youth and Family Services
  One South Montgomery Street
  Trenton, NJ 08625
    Reports made to (800) 792-8610. District offices also
  provide 24-hour telephone services.

New Mexico:
  New Mexico Department of Human Services
  P.O. Box 2348
  Santa Fe, NM 87503
    Reports made to County Social Services Offices or to
  (800) 432-6217.

New York:
  New York Division of Family and Children Services
  Department of Social Services
  Child Protective Services
  40 North Pearl Street
  Albany, NY 12243
    Reports made to (800) 342-3720 or to District Offices.

North Carolina:
North Carolina Department of Human Resources
Division of Social Services
325 North Salisbury Street
Raleigh, NC 27611
Reports made to County Departments of Social Services.

North Dakota:
North Dakota Department of Human Services
Social Services Division
Children and Family Services Unit
Child Abuse and Neglect Program
Russel Building, Hwy. 83 North
Bismarck, ND 58505
Reports made to Board of Social Services Area Offices and to 24-hour reporting services provided by Human Services Centers.

Ohio:
Ohio Department of Public Welfare
Bureau of Child Protective Services
30 East Board Street
Columbus, OH 43215
Reports made to County Departments of Public Welfare.

Oklahoma:
Oklahoma Department of Institutions, Social and Rehabilitative Services
Division of Child Welfare
P.O. Box 25352
Oklahoma City, OK 73125
Reports made to (800) 522-3511.

Oregon:
   Department of Human Services
   Children's Services Division
   Protective Services
   509 Public Services Building
   Salem, OR 97310
      Reports made to local Children's Services Division
   Offices and to (503) 378-3016.

Pennsylvania:
   Pennsylvania Department of Public Welfare
   Office of Children, Youth and Families
   Bureau of Family and Community Programs
   Child Line and Abuse Registry
   Lanco Lodge, P.O. 2675
   Harrisburg, PA 17102
      Reports made to the toll-free CHILDLINE (800)
   932-0313.

Puerto Rico:
   Puerto Rico Department of Social Services
   Services to Family With Children
   P.O. Box 11398
   Fernandez Juncos Station
   Santurez, PR 00910
      Reports made to local offices or to the Department.

Rhode Island:
   Rhode Island Department of Children and Families
   610 Mt. Pleasant Avenue, Bldg. #7
   Providence, RI 02908
      Reports made to State agency child protective services
   unit at (800) 662-5100 or to District Offices.

South Carolina:
  South Carolina Department of Social Services
  1535 Confederate Avenue
  Columbia, SC 29202
    Reports made to County Departments of Social
  Services.

South Dakota:
  Department of Social Services
  Office of Children, Youth and Family Services
  700 North Illinois Street
  Pierre, SD 57501
    Reports made to local offices.

Tennessee:
  Tennessee Department of Human Services
  Child Protective Services
  State Office Building
  Nashville, TN 37219
    Reports made to County Departments of Human
  Services.

Texas:
  Texas Department of Human Resources
  Protective Services for Children Branch
  P.O. Box 2960, MC 537-A
  Austin, TX 78769
    Reports made to (800) 252-5400.

Utah:
  Department of Social Services
  Division of Family Services
  P.O. Box 2500
  Salt Lake City, UT 84110
    Reports made to Division of Family Services District
  Offices.

Vermont:
> Vermont Department of Social and Rehabilitative
> Services
> Division of Social Services
> 103 South Main Street
> Waterbury, VT 05676
>> Reports made to State agency at (800) 828-3422 or to
>> District Offices (24-hour services).

Virgin Islands:
> Virgin Islands Department of Social Welfare
> Division of Social Services
> P.O. Box 500
> Charlotte Amalie
> St. Thomas, VI 00801
>> Reports made to the Division of Social Services.

Virginia:
> Virginia Department of Welfare
> Bureau of Family and Community Programs
> 8007 Discovery Drive
> Richmond, VA 23288
>> Reports made to (800) 552-7096 in Virginia, and (804)
>> 281-9081 outside the state.

Washington:
> Department of Social and Health Services
> Community Services Division
> Child Protective Services
> Mail Stop OB 41-D
> Olympia, WA 98504
>> Reports made to local Social and Health Services
>> Offices.

West Virginia:
  West Virginia Department of Human Services
  Division of Social Services
  Child Protective Services
  State Office Building
  Charleston, WV 25305
    Reports made to (800) 352-6513.

Wisconsin:
  Wisconsin Department of Health and Social Services
  Division of Community Services
  Office of Children, Youth, and Families
  1 West Wilson Street
  Madison, WI
    Reports made to County Social Services Office.

Wyoming:
  Department of Health and Social Services
  Division of Public Assistance and Social Services
  Hathaway Building
  Cheyenne, WY 82002
    Reports made to County Departments of Public
  Assistance and Social Services.

National Organizations Concerned with Child Abuse and
Neglect:

Action for Child Protection
202 E Street, NW
Washington, DC 20002
(202) 393-1090

American Humane Association
9725 East Hampden Avenue
Denver, CO 80231
(303) 695-0811

C. Henry Kempe Center for Prevention and Treatment of
    Child Abuse and Neglect
1205 Oneida Street
Denver, CO 80220
(303) 321-3963

Child Welfare League of America
440 1st Street, NW
Washington, DC 20001
(202) 638-2952

Childhelp USA
6463 Independence Avenue
Woodland Hills, CA 91367
Hotline: 1-800-4-A-CHILD or 1-800-422-4453
    (Referrals to services and resources in every state are
provided 24 hours a day, 7 days a week.)

National Center for Child Abuse and Neglect (NCCAN)
P.O. Box 1182
Washington, DC 20013
(301) 251-5157

National Center for Missing and Exploited Children
1835 K Street, NW
Washington, DC 20006
(202) 634-9821

National Committee for Prevention of Child Abuse
332 South Michigan Avenue
Chicago, IL 60604
(312) 663-3520

APPENDIX   129

National Exchange Club Foundation for Prevention of
   Child Abuse
3050 Central Avenue
Toledo, OH 43606
(419) 535-3232

National Network of Runaway and Youth Services
905 6th Street, NW
Washington, DC 20024
(202) 488-0739

Parents Anonymous
7120 Franklin Avenue
Los Angeles, CA 90046
(800) 421-0353
   (Referrals to local self-help groups for parents and
children.)

Parents United/Daughters and Sons United/Adults Molested as Children United
P.O. Box 952
San Jose, CA 95108
(408) 280-5055
   (National self-help groups for families with sexual abuse
problems. They sponsor groups throughout the country
for children, teens, parents, and adults molested as
children.)

Canadian Resources

Provincial Services:

BRITISH COLUMBIA
Ministry of Human Resources
(604) 387-4411

ALBERTA
Child Welfare Authorities
(403) 266-8849

MANITOBA
Children's Aid Society
(204) 942-0511

SASKATCHEWAN
Social Services Department
(306) 565-3504

ONTARIO
Children's Aid Society
(416) 924-4646

QUEBEC
Ville Marie Social Services
(514) 989-1781

NEW BRUNSWICK
Department of Social Services
(506) 658-2536

NOVA SCOTIA
Department of Social Services
(902) 425-5420

NEWFOUNDLAND
Department of Social Services
(709) 596-5054

National Resources:

Abducted Child Rights of Canada
(406) 498-5835

Canadian Society for the Prevention of Cruelty to Children
(705) 526-5647

Catholic Children's Aid Society
(416) 925-6641

Citizens Concerned with Crime Against Children
(519) 439-4226

Index

A

absent spouse, 56-58
abuse, physical, 19, 28, 37, 44,
  53, 55-56, 63, 68, 91
abuser, sexual
  accepting responsibility, 87
  avoiding, 92
  as childhood victim, 10,
    100-101
  confrontation with, 78
  described, 9-11
  known to victim, 4, 7, 13-14
  vs. molester, 6-7
  / molester combination, 7-8
  and promises to stop, 89-90
access, of abuser to victim, 4, 9,
  41-42
activity, sexual
  forced, 25, 57
  minor in, 2, 5, 45, 61
  premature, 72, 75
adolescent, as abuser, viii, 95-104
adult
  as childhood victim, 67
  insomnia in, 69
  talking with responsible, 2
affection
  need for, 13, 15, 42, 58
  shown to victim, 28
AIDS, 20
alcohol abuse, 16, 20, 52-53, 63,
  68, 70, 99
anger
  abuser's feelings of, 10, 23, 46,
    58, 101
  family's, at victim, 35

at mother, 32, 34, 70, 79
at self, 70
victim's, at abuser, 45, 70, 81
anorexia nervosa, 70
aunt, as abuser, 4, 27, 37
authority, abuser as person in, 3,
  9, 10, 13

B

baby-sitter, as abuser, 3, 9,
  96-97
behavior
  delinquent, 20
  difficulties, adolescent, 19,
    23-24
  emulating adult, 15
  rationalizing, 61
  regressive, 58
  self-abusive, 70
  sexually abusive, 2, 3-4, 15
betrayal, by sibling, 98
Bible, and sexual references, 17
blackmail, emotional, 6
blended family, 49
books, use in counseling, 77
boyfriend/girlfriend, parent's, 14,
  43, 49
boys as victims, 25, 39-48
bulimia, 70

C

characteristics
  of abusers, 9, 100-101